I0002102

The Science of Artificial Intelligence – Part 5 – Mastering the Probabilistic Learning Surface

By Michael
Sinyangwe
In 2021

NOTA BENE: If any organisation/individual wants to use any of the natural language text, code, tables, or images, in this Obsidian Oblation book (or any similar such things) in any of their internal/external books/products/services/experiences, then they must agree to, and are indeed bound by the Almighty God under Wrath of punishment, to do the following 3 things: 1. Make reference to me (actual name, Literary name (Caramel Cocoa Brownie), and Obsidian Oblation... logo optional) as the originator of core natural language text, code, tables, or images in the internal/external book/product/service/experience, within the internal/external book/product/service/experience itself in a prominent position; 2. Make ongoing total monthly donations of 1% of all income{costs plus contingent}/revenue (whichever is greatest) generated by all of your internal/external books/products/services/Experiences which use any of the natural language text, code, tables, or images in this Obsidian Oblation book (or any similar such things), to any Catholic Charities of your choice who are part of the Catholic Church's Obsidian Caritas Social Action Network of official Catholic Charities; 3. Include this nota bene in a prominent position in all documentation/code scripts that use any of the natural language text, code, tables, or images in this Obsidian Oblation book (or any similar such things)... Moreover, if you use any ideas, concepts, or algorithmic designs within this Obsidian Oblation book, that are conveyed to you in non-computer code language (e.g. natural human language or images etc.), in any of your internal/external books/products/services/experiences, then I strongly exhort you to donate that 1% of total ongoing income{costs plus contingent}/revenue generated, to any Catholic Charities of your choice who are part of the Catholic Church's Obsidian Caritas Social Action Network of official Catholic Charities. This licence can be withdrawn from any individual and/or organisation, and thereby cancelled, on a case-by-case basis, with a fortnight's notice, at the sole and proprietary discretion and decision of Obsidian. Also, Obsidian and its owners and employees, accept no liabilities whatsoever, for the use of anything contained herein this book, nor any of its derivatives.

Contents

Probability Theory Introduction

This book outlines my core probability theories. Somewhat tested, but most likely not infallible. This theory is intended to help with distribution learning, specifically around prioritising a set of options, or future state projection scenarios. It includes, and rolls up all the other machine learning books that I have published, including a mention of the Part 3 – Mastering the Sequential Learning Surface content, which can be found demonstrated in T-SQL source-code on my GitHub account (Scarlett-Pimpernell). This is essentially the whole stack of digital machine learning complete now. All that is left out is the actual decisioning technique, which should be coded to run off deterministic, explicit, and largely static If/Then/Else programming logic, which sits on top of the full stack, and in so doing, completes it.

The Machine Learning Algorithm Stack

1. Decision Science - Obsidian Ranking If/Then/Else 'Learning' (Core Tech Researched).
2. Option Science - Michaelian Probability Learning (Core Tech Researched).
3. Causal Science- Causal Model Learning (Core Tech Ideated).

4. Search Science - Transformer Ranking Vector Learning (Core Tech Researched).
5. Perception Science - Deep Sensual Network Learning (Core Tech Theorised).
6. Component Science - Deep Reinforcement Learning (Core Tech Researched).

Essentially, there are two core machine learning algorithms left to research and develop, each with a dependency on a crucial new/disruptive technology, before reaching level 1 of 4 artificial general intelligence (AGI), of which there are multiple levels themselves. They are in fact "two sides of the same coin". As mentioned in my book entitled: "The Theory of Everything Equation - Projecting Any Future", these core machine learning algorithms are:

1. Fundamental Science - Abstraction Learning - Quantum State Identification Measurement (2030s).
2. Essential Science - Extraction Learning - Lattice Wave Resonance Emergence (2040s).

Michaelian Probability Theory

Whenever you have a dataset, the mean average allows you to calculate the **percentile effect** across the dataset, according to the law of normal distribution curves, which automatically applies to any dataset where a mean average can be calculated. The percentile effect simply describes the fact that as you project future states further and further away from the mean average, the probability of that projection being correct increasingly reduces near the mean average, and then decreasingly reduces towards the dataset limits, thereby creating the mirrored s-curve either side of the mean average. The shape, i.e. height and width, of this normal distribution curve is dictated by dataset significance (or spread). The existence of duplicate sample parameters simply multiplies the underlying confidence of probability, and thereby introduces humps (or modalities) to the normal distribution curve. In between these modalities, there are density depression ranges where probability reduces. Finally, there is a need to allow for a sense of granularity around each parameter in order to generate probability peaks within the overall normal distribution curve. An additional set of **similarity metrics** are also provided in the source code below.

Nota Bene: Traditional probability theory assumes an un-skewed normal distribution. This outdated probability theory also omits the reality of parameter density, and so can't accommodate multi-modality either. As such, my following probability theory is superior. It both handles distribution skew and density with ease, and should outperform traditional probability on the vast majority of applied real-world solutions, which usually deal with skewed and mostly sparse datasets!

<u>You can find an example T-SQL query covering all the following significance and confidence calculations, on my GitHub account (Scarlett-Pimpernell).</u>

The Michaelian Probability SQL Server 2019, T-SQL Source Code
--HEADER:

--MS Obsidian Michaelian Pseudo-Quantum Probability Distribution Algorithm (Called a Variational Auto-Encoder)

--SQL Server 2019

--T-SQL

--Collation: Latin1_General_CI_AS

--Initial Operating Capability

--Version 1.96

--OVERVIEW:

--TraditFional Bayesian probability theory assumes an 'un-skewed' normal distribution. This outdated Bayesian probability theory also omits the reality of parameter density, and so can't accommodate multi-modality either. As such, my following Michaelian pseudo-quantum probability theory is superior. It both handles distribution skew and density with ease, and should outperform traditional Bayesian probability on the vast majority of applied real-world solutions, which usually deal with skewed and mostly sparse datasets!

--The following Michaelian pseudo-quantum probability distribution algorithm, can be used advantageously for numerous purposes, some of which include:

--1. As part of the core AGI Level 1 corpus of machine learning theory and research that I have made available on Amazon (Michael Sinyangwe) and GitHub (Scarlett-Pimpernell).

--2. If you are looking to use an existing machine learning model in order to solve a problem in your domain, which has its own unique population characteristics, it is often beneficial to comparatively analyse a representative sample from both populations, before re-purposing and deployment, in order to ascertain an understanding of dataset ('population') similarity.

--3. Checking dataset similarity in order to sample only the weights and embeddings of a trained machine learning model that are most ideal for re-use with your dataset (and therefore problem space), and thereby reduces time-to-solution, cost-of-solution, and pollution-from-solution, while most likely improving effectiveness.

--4. You can also apply the projection distribution mesh search transformations directly to raw dataset parameters, in order to get native rather than normalised probabilities, and in fact, this will probably be a more common usage for this algorithm.

--5. Michaelian similarities can also be used to analyse bias in ML datasets.

--6. You could also use the fully normalised datasets table variable in this algorithm to simply correct for differential dataset contextual features such as lighting conditions across a set of different video feeds, or maybe where other re-contextualised quantitative signature comparisons are needed etc.

--7. Multi-dimensional probabilistic optimisation, where each axial scalar pool for the input variable has its own probability metrics calculated (usually spot or spread confidence), and then the outputs are constructed into a multi-dimensional graph, where local and global minimas, maximas, and inflexions can be easily extracted.

--8. You could turn this query into a SQL Server function, and then build Michaelian Pseudo-Quantum Probability Distribution Deep Neural Nets with it... just an option.... I call this concept the Feed-Upward Neural Network

--9. The similarity matrices can be easily utilised for semi-supervised auto-labelling of, for example, graph traces, or images/photos.

--10. A digital reliability twin of the enterprise... Tracking one or more performance metrics (min/avg/max over the last x seconds/minutes/hours/days), per unit of tech asset (hardware or software), in terms of confidence and significance probabilities... As a manager, I would like to know for example the real-time power consumption of a computer server or factory machine, so that I can spot exceptional operating behaviour which could lead to an issue, problem, or failure (maybe also aggregating into MTBI, MTBP, and MTBF)... In this way, I can avoid unnecessary costs to the enterprise.

--11. A forward stimulus for the attention of fame and money hungry machine learning enthusiasts... Future forms of causal machine learning will almost certainly include this Michaelian distribution similarity metric as part of their algorithm!

--USAGE DIRECTIONS:

--First set appropriate global variables for your particular analysis. See the guidelines in the comments adjacent to the assignations in the source code below.

--Then check to make sure that all the values in the parameter column in your input CSV file, have had thousand separator commas removed (e.g. 1,750,000.33 becomes 1750000.33).

--Then copy the appropriate CSV file into the filepath folder.

--After this, your query is ready to execute, so long as you have enabled permissions to create SQL Server functions for your SQL Server user, and also Windows permissions to open/read files from the assigned file import directory (see global variables in this query) for your Windows user.

--FUNCTIONALITY STILL TO BE INCLUDED IN THE ALGORITHM INCLUDES:

--All IOC version functionality delivered.

--TESTING:

--Unit Tests To Be Carried Out By Each Developer In Order To Satisfy That the Theory Has Been Correctly Applied.

--Handles negative and zero parameters appropriately.

--Maximal confidence of <=100%, and minimal confidence >=0%, where there is actually a fundamental distribution (i.e. where there are more than 2 unique parameter values in the dataset).

--Correct distribution profile for smaller and larger datasets e.g. 80 samples and 800 samples aswell.

--Correctly skewed density peaks (parameters) and troughs (gaps).

--Large low density sub-ranges >=0%.

--Incorporation of overall distribution skewness.

--Density depressions should have a severity which is relative to the density depression range.

--When median and mean are the same, i.e. where no skew exists, that mean confidence is a distribution maxima, because the dataset is fundamentally symmetrical, and also the mean should be the maxima given a 50% granularity.

--As sample dataset becomes more diverse (i.e. as significance increases), so total integral should increase, because the distribution is essentially spreading out more, and therefore covering a greater 2-dimensional area.

--Zero confidence dataset range when only two unique parameter values exist across the samples (pseudo-binary probability), because fundamentally there is not really a distribution unless you have a minimum of 3 unique parameter values.

--Your code produces the same values as those in the tables above, given the same variable parameters as the input dataset, and the same global variables, because I am correct.

--Estimated query execution time with my SSD, 8GB RAM, 8-core 2.0 Base GHz: 4.0 Boost GHz laptop, with an install of SQL Server Express where the licence is restricting execution to a single core with 1GB RAM, using typical global variables of 1% for @Target_Deepset_Training_Significance, 50% for @Parameter_Granularity_Global_Variable_Perc entage, and 1% for @Projection_Granularity_Global_Variable_Perc entage, on an input CSV file with 5 datasets, each with 200 parameters: IS ABOUT 1 MINUTE.

--Microsoft Azure Cloud currently (in 2021) offers SSD, 80-core Azure SQL Server Instances which would reduce this query time to most likely below 5 seconds for those who desire to deploy the query within high throughput applications, with minor adjustments to the source code.

--NOTA BENE:

--This query is only intended for use with ASCII printable characters in the input CSV file.

--The original column headers from the CSV template file called Datasets_For_Michaelian_Probability_Analysis (available alongside this query on my GitHub account Scarlett-Pimpernell), must be retained within the CSV. The first column header is Dataset, and the second column header is Parameter.

--Beware that this algorithm includes the likely possibility for curve discontinuities to arise. This is intended behaviour in the realm of pseudo-quantum michaelian probability, and especially desirable when your application requires high levels of precision.

--There are at least 3 showstopper table variable joining bugs (they may be the same underlying bug) in my current version of SQL Server 2019. It misses a join for >= operator. Also, there are 2 grouped aggregate count having clause showstopper bugs also in the core SQL Server 2019 engine. Please see comments in the source code below. As a result, I advise you, please don't deploy this algorithm to production, until Microsoft has been alerted, and the bug fixed!

--For typical use assumed as up to 10 datasets, each with up to 1,000 parameters, this query should be pretty rapid, even on a single core.

--The datasets provided as inputs must only contain dataset labels which are text data type i.e. have at least one non-numeric character, and parameter values which are numeric (either integer or decimal).

--The maximum usable CSV input file character count is just under 2 billion characters (not including control or extended ASCII characters). You could of course adjust the query appropriately if you have a big data application such as physics simulators or financial modellers etc, but really, you should simply be sampling your parameters properly!... and if you do use this query for very large datasets or very large numbers of datasets, it is almost necessary that you purchase an appropriate highly multi-core SQL Server license, along with appropriate hardware either in the cloud, or on premises.

--The maximum dataset name length is 250 characters, but of course, you could easily change this.

--You could convert all table variables to memory optimised tables, in order to speed up the query, given suitable RAM resources, however otherwise, this would likely impact data volume limits.

--This query assumes that you definitely won't ever get the string pattern ×¬¯ in your dataset names. When implementing in your own product or service, please remember to check each dataset string for this string pattern before importing, and take appropriate action. If this string pattern will be in your input data, then choose a different and more appropriate binding string pattern... possibly longer, and definitely with other and/or more binding characters.

--You will only get a curve almost touching 100% confidence with a setting of 50% parameter granularity, when the dataset mid-range is in the parameter values. Otherwise the mid-range peak will actually be a density depression.

--Just reminding users that they would be wise to make sure that the parameter granularity global variable is constant across analysis instances that they wish to compare in a post-hoc fashion.

--The @Limit_Normalised_Projection_Spot_Confidence_Percentage transformation is very parallel-compute and RAM intensive. If you do not have enough of these resources, execution time is exponentially increased, and indeed may never complete.

--Finally, the midpoint spot confidence at 50% parameter granularity will never reach 100%. The reason is referred to as the long-tail problem. Basically, the spread (different from spot) confidence at the midpoint, with a 50% parameter granularity, gives you the hopefully infinitessimal probabity that your next observation will be outside the current dataset range, and therefore is likely subject to a significantly different system of probabilistic distribution.

--INITIATION:

Set NoExec Off --If this is not executed, the query may under some circumstances not complete repeat executions after a CSV data input validation check fails.

Select ('Query Started At Around:' + Cast(GetDate() As Nvarchar(Max))) As [Execution_Progress]

--GLOBAL VARIABLES:

Declare @File_Directory Nvarchar(200)

Set @File_Directory = 'C:\TEMP\Obsidian_Michaelian_Probability'

Set @File_Directory = (Case When Right(@File_Directory, 1) = '\' Then @File_Directory Else (@File_Directory + '\') End) --The case statement is used in order to always make sure that the file path includes a trailing backslash (\).

--This file path variable tells the query what directory your input CSV file is saved in.

Declare @File_Name Nvarchar(50)

Set @File_Name = 'Datasets_For_Michaelian_Probability_Analysis'

Set @File_Name = (Case When Right(@File_Name, 4) = '.csv' Then @File_Name Else (@File_Name + '.csv') End) --The case statement is used in order to always make sure that the file name includes a trailing extension (.csv).

--This file name variable tells the query what file you wish to import for analysis.

Declare @Outlier_Threshold_Percentage Float

Set @Outlier_Threshold_Percentage = 50

--This outlier threshold global variable must be restricted to (0% < x <= 100%).

--It determines outlier band exclusions later on.

--Essentially if there are not at least two other parameters within the outlier percentage threshold of a given parameter, the parameter is excluded from the analysis.

--Ideally, you want to set this global variable to around 50% in my opinion, but could vary this to at least as low as 20% depending on the application.

Declare @Target_Deepset_Training_Significance Float

Set @Target_Deepset_Training_Significance = 1

--This significance global variable must be restricted to (0% < x <= 33.33%)... Alternatively, convert this global variable to Sigma-Band Labels instead (may be more intuitive for the end-user, but you sacrifice useful specificity).

--It is used in an observation/parameter reduction technique later on, in order to improve computational speed/efficiency. Afterall, it is not necessary to include all parameters in the training/transformation stage, because this algorithm is an interpolating generative optimiser... It can estimate the parameter gaps/blanks with a high degree of fidelity.

--Essentially, the percentage value assigned here, decides the Significance of the analysis, in accord with the sigma scale outlined in my Data

Science Theory book, which is published on Amazon.

--Ideally, you want to set this global variable to a significance of between 1% (most speedy/efficient) and 0.000001% (least speedy/efficient).

Declare
@Parameter_Granularity_Global_Variable_Perc entage Float

Set
@Parameter_Granularity_Global_Variable_Perc entage = 50

--This parameter granularity global variable must be restricted to (0% =< x <= 50%), and is used in order to set the duplicate count lookup range. It thereby effectively broadens curve peaks as desired for a given application of the theory. For example, you would want wider normal distribution curve peaks if you need greater accuracy of probability. This can be achieved by using a higher parameter granularity percentage. On the other hand, you would want narrower normal distribution curve peaks if you instead need greater precision of probability. This can be achieved by using a lower parameter granularity percentage. The recommended value for this global variable is anywhere between 10% and 50%. A value of 50% would super-nominally simulate the classical normal distribution curve either side of the mean, which originates from the older Bayesian probability theory. But be aware, that the higher the parameter granularity %, the less skew your model will be able to exhibit.

Declare @Projection_Granularity_Global_Variable_Percentage Float

Set @Projection_Granularity_Global_Variable_Percentage = 1

--This projection granularity global variable must ideally be restricted to (0.000001% =< x <= 10%), with 1% being roughly optimal in order to obtain a lean analysis. This value is used in order to set the distribution mesh search transformation gap.

--Please remember to sufficiently search the dataset range distribution space. Your set of scenario projection datapoints should start at the range minima, finish at the range maxima, and have no more than a 10% dataset range gap between any two members, and ideally a lot less. If you do not sufficiently search the probability space, then the resulting confidence percentages will be sub-optimal. Also, beware, if you are experiencing an exploding sigmoid curve as your dataset becomes highly polarised, then this algorithm is not suitable for your dataset. The best approach in this case, would be to use a pool-sized ternary probability algorithm, which is effectively achieved via the @Limit_Normalised_Projection_Spot_Confidence_Percentage table variable transformation. This ternary algorithm allows us to flatten any gradient explosion to the outer probability value. Ternary probability... Exploding depressions are limit normalised down to the low-density probability curve inner trough midpoint, while exploding peaks are limit normalised down to the high-density probability curve outer edge parameter. The trick to ascertaining whether you have an exploding gradient is as follows. If any 2 ordered parameters have a gap between them which is at least 80% of the dataset range, then I would suppose it is likely that your model is at least starting to experience an exploding gradient issue.

--The lower the projection granularity, the exponentially slower the algorithm. In fact, values below 0.1% are unadvisable.

Declare
@Exploding_Probability_Gradient_Dataset_Ran
ge_Limit_Percentage Float

Set
@Exploding_Probability_Gradient_Dataset_Ran
ge_Limit_Percentage = 50

--This variable must be limited to within the
range of values (0% < x < 92%).

--92% upper limit, because much greater than
this, and SQL Server cannot currently calculate
and store the massive gradient explosion values
that could otherwise result. This inherent
lacking in SQL Server might dismay some black
hole theoretical physicists!

--I rceommend that the value of this global
variable is initially set to somewhere around
50% (not sure why, could be wrong, but just
seems to work okay during development, but
would need a scientific study to reach the
optimal value) in situations where optimisation
of this variable is not possible. Experience
indicates that greater than this starts to miss
instances of significant gradient explosion, and
less than this starts to indiscriminately limit the
probability distribution curve when it is
unnecessary.

--Also I would suggest a value for this variable which is within 50% (scaled, not literal) of the parameter granularity global variable, because otherwise this creates a model variable colliding mismatch, where there is unnecessary asymmetric variable granularity. This variable asymmetry impedes the full action potential of one or the other of the variables. As I have said, I am currently unable to provide guidance on the best value for this variable given the various contextual situations that you may be modelling, and so I highly recommend that you either randomly search the allowed values for this variable for the optimal value, or it may probably be better to perform a mesh search of the allowed variable range.

--As far as I can tell, setting this global variable for gradient explosion limits, below 20% would be superfluous.

--If you want a 'maximally' smoothed curve, then set this exploding gradient limit global variable to 92%.

Declare @CSV_Column_Delimiter Nvarchar(1)

Set @CSV_Column_Delimiter = ','

--A comma column Delimiter is highly recommended here, because I have not 'fully' tested with other Delimiters (although basic tests seemed to work fine with other Delimiters). If you do use a different column Delimiter other than a comma, please test thoroughly!

--TYPES, VIEWS, AND FUNCTIONS:

--The following few blocks of code create a new function which is used later on in this query in order to generate a table variable with 1 column containing increasing integers.

Declare @Create_Function_Command Nvarchar(Max);

Set @Create_Function_Command =

        N'Create Function dbo.Element_Index_Generator_Code(@Index_ Count BigInt)

Returns Nvarchar(Max)

With Returns Null On Null Input

As

Begin

Declare @Element_Index_Generator_Code Nvarchar(Max)

Set @Element_Index_Generator_Code =

(Case When @Index_Count < 1 Then "Null"

Else (Case When @Index_Count > 999999999 Then "Null"

Else (Case When @Index_Count <= 9 Then "Select Singles(n) As [Element_Index] From (Values(0),(1),(2),(3),(4),(5),(6),(7),(8),(9)) Singles(n) Where Singles.n <= @Index_Count"

Else (Case When @Index_Count <= 99 Then "Select Singles.n + 10*Tens.n As [Element_Index] From (Values(0),(1),(2),(3),(4),(5),(6),(7),(8),(9)) Singles(n), (Values(0),(1),(2),(3),(4),(5),(6),(7),(8),(9))

Tens(n) Where Singles.n + 10*Tens.n <=
@Index_Count"

Else (Case When @Index_Count <= 999 Then
"Select Singles.n + 10*Tens.n + 100*Hundreds.n
As [Element_Index] From
(Values(0),(1),(2),(3),(4),(5),(6),(7),(8),(9))
Singles(n),
(Values(0),(1),(2),(3),(4),(5),(6),(7),(8),(9))
Tens(n),
(Values(0),(1),(2),(3),(4),(5),(6),(7),(8),(9))
Hundreds(n) Where Singles.n + 10*Tens.n +
100*Hundreds.n <= @Index_Count"

Else (Case When @Index_Count <= 9999 Then
"Select Singles.n + 10*Tens.n + 100*Hundreds.n
+ 1000*Thousands.n As [Element_Index] From
(Values(0),(1),(2),(3),(4),(5),(6),(7),(8),(9))
Singles(n),
(Values(0),(1),(2),(3),(4),(5),(6),(7),(8),(9))
Tens(n),
(Values(0),(1),(2),(3),(4),(5),(6),(7),(8),(9))
Hundreds(n),
(Values(0),(1),(2),(3),(4),(5),(6),(7),(8),(9))
Thousands(n) Where Singles.n + 10*Tens.n +
100*Hundreds.n + 1000*Thousands.n <=
@Index_Count"

Else (Case When @Index_Count <= 99999 Then
"Select Singles.n + 10*Tens.n + 100*Hundreds.n
+ 1000*Thousands.n + 10000*TenThousands.n

As [Element_Index] From
(Values(0),(1),(2),(3),(4),(5),(6),(7),(8),(9))
Singles(n),
(Values(0),(1),(2),(3),(4),(5),(6),(7),(8),(9))
Tens(n),
(Values(0),(1),(2),(3),(4),(5),(6),(7),(8),(9))
Hundreds(n),
(Values(0),(1),(2),(3),(4),(5),(6),(7),(8),(9))
Thousands(n),
(Values(0),(1),(2),(3),(4),(5),(6),(7),(8),(9))
TenThousands(n) Where Singles.n + 10*Tens.n
+ 100*Hundreds.n + 1000*Thousands.n +
10000*TenThousands.n <= @Index_Count''

Else (Case When @Index_Count <= 999999
Then ''Select Singles.n + 10*Tens.n +
100*Hundreds.n + 1000*Thousands.n +
10000*TenThousands.n +
100000*HundredThousands.n As
[Element_Index] From
(Values(0),(1),(2),(3),(4),(5),(6),(7),(8),(9))
Singles(n),
(Values(0),(1),(2),(3),(4),(5),(6),(7),(8),(9))
Tens(n),
(Values(0),(1),(2),(3),(4),(5),(6),(7),(8),(9))
Hundreds(n),
(Values(0),(1),(2),(3),(4),(5),(6),(7),(8),(9))
Thousands(n),
(Values(0),(1),(2),(3),(4),(5),(6),(7),(8),(9))
TenThousands(n),

(Values(0),(1),(2),(3),(4),(5),(6),(7),(8),(9))
HundredThousands(n) Where Singles.n +
10*Tens.n + 100*Hundreds.n +
1000*Thousands.n + 10000*TenThousands.n +
100000*HundredThousands.n <=
@Index_Count"

Else (Case When @Index_Count <= 9999999
Then "Select Singles.n + 10*Tens.n +
100*Hundreds.n + 1000*Thousands.n +
10000*TenThousands.n +
100000*HundredThousands.n +
1000000*Millions.n As [Element_Index] From
(Values(0),(1),(2),(3),(4),(5),(6),(7),(8),(9))
Singles(n),
(Values(0),(1),(2),(3),(4),(5),(6),(7),(8),(9))
Tens(n),
(Values(0),(1),(2),(3),(4),(5),(6),(7),(8),(9))
Hundreds(n),
(Values(0),(1),(2),(3),(4),(5),(6),(7),(8),(9))
Thousands(n),
(Values(0),(1),(2),(3),(4),(5),(6),(7),(8),(9))
TenThousands(n),
(Values(0),(1),(2),(3),(4),(5),(6),(7),(8),(9))
HundredThousands(n),
(Values(0),(1),(2),(3),(4),(5),(6),(7),(8),(9))
Millions(n) Where Singles.n + 10*Tens.n +
100*Hundreds.n + 1000*Thousands.n +
10000*TenThousands.n +

```
100000*HundredThousands.n +
1000000*Millions.n <= @Index_Count"

Else (Case When @Index_Count <= 99999999
Then "Select Singles.n + 10*Tens.n +
100*Hundreds.n + 1000*Thousands.n +
10000*TenThousands.n +
100000*HundredThousands.n +
1000000*Millions.n + 10000000*TenMillions.n
As [Element_Index] From
(Values(0),(1),(2),(3),(4),(5),(6),(7),(8),(9))
Singles(n),
(Values(0),(1),(2),(3),(4),(5),(6),(7),(8),(9))
Tens(n),
(Values(0),(1),(2),(3),(4),(5),(6),(7),(8),(9))
Hundreds(n),
(Values(0),(1),(2),(3),(4),(5),(6),(7),(8),(9))
Thousands(n),
(Values(0),(1),(2),(3),(4),(5),(6),(7),(8),(9))
TenThousands(n),
(Values(0),(1),(2),(3),(4),(5),(6),(7),(8),(9))
HundredThousands(n),
(Values(0),(1),(2),(3),(4),(5),(6),(7),(8),(9))
Millions(n),
(Values(0),(1),(2),(3),(4),(5),(6),(7),(8),(9))
TenMillions(n) Where Singles.n + 10*Tens.n +
100*Hundreds.n + 1000*Thousands.n +
10000*TenThousands.n +
100000*HundredThousands.n +
```

1000000*Millions.n + 10000000*TenMillions.n
<= @Index_Count"

Else "Select Singles.n + 10*Tens.n +
100*Hundreds.n + 1000*Thousands.n +
10000*TenThousands.n +
100000*HundredThousands.n +
1000000*Millions.n + 10000000*TenMillions.n
+ 100000000*HundredMillions.n As
[Element_Index] From
(Values(0),(1),(2),(3),(4),(5),(6),(7),(8),(9))
Singles(n),
(Values(0),(1),(2),(3),(4),(5),(6),(7),(8),(9))
Tens(n),
(Values(0),(1),(2),(3),(4),(5),(6),(7),(8),(9))
Hundreds(n),
(Values(0),(1),(2),(3),(4),(5),(6),(7),(8),(9))
Thousands(n),
(Values(0),(1),(2),(3),(4),(5),(6),(7),(8),(9))
TenThousands(n),
(Values(0),(1),(2),(3),(4),(5),(6),(7),(8),(9))
HundredThousands(n),
(Values(0),(1),(2),(3),(4),(5),(6),(7),(8),(9))
Millions(n),
(Values(0),(1),(2),(3),(4),(5),(6),(7),(8),(9))
TenMillions(n),
(Values(0),(1),(2),(3),(4),(5),(6),(7),(8),(9))
HundredMillions(n) Where Singles.n +
10*Tens.n + 100*Hundreds.n +
1000*Thousands.n + 10000*TenThousands.n +

```
100000*HundredThousands.n +
1000000*Millions.n + 10000000*TenMillions.n
+ 100000000*HundredMillions.n <=
@Index_Count"

End) End) End) End) End) End) End) End) End)
End)


Return @Element_Index_Generator_Code


End';
```

If Not Exists (Select * From Sysobjects Where Name='Element_Index_Generator_Code' and Xtype='FN') --Make sure this function is not in use for another proprietary technique outside the Quantum Encryption repository.

```
Execute sp_executesql
@Create_Function_Command;
```

--EXTRACTION STAGE:

```
Select ('Extraction Stage Started At Around:' +
Cast(GetDate() As Nvarchar(Max))) As
[Execution_Progress]
```

--The following codeblocks extract data from a CSV file in your previously assigned import directory (see global variables near the beginning of this query).

```
Declare @File_Path Nvarchar(250)

Set @File_Path = (@File_Directory +
@File_Name)

Declare @Dynamic_SQL_1 Nvarchar(Max)

Set @Dynamic_SQL_1 = N'Select * From
Openrowset(Bulk ''' + @File_Path + ''',
Single_Clob) As Data'

Declare
@Dynamic_SQL_Parameter_Definition_1
Nvarchar(Max)
```

```
Set @Dynamic_SQL_Parameter_Definition_1 =
N'@Parameter_1 Nvarchar(250)'


Declare
@Dynamic_SQL_Intermediate_Table_Variable_
1 Table ([Data] Nvarchar(Max))

Insert Into
@Dynamic_SQL_Intermediate_Table_Variable_
1 ([Data])

Execute sp_executesql @Dynamic_SQL_1,
@Dynamic_SQL_Parameter_Definition_1,
@Parameter_1 = @File_Path



--The following codeblocks transform data from
the CSV file into inputs for the Michaelian
pseudo-quantum probability analysis

Declare @Raw_Datasets_Intermediate Table
([Value] Nvarchar(Max))

Insert Into @Raw_Datasets_Intermediate
([Value])

Select Value From String_Split((Select
Replace([Data], ('Dataset, Parameter' +
Char(13)), '') From
```

```
@Dynamic_SQL_Intermediate_Table_Variable_
1), Char(13))


Declare @Raw_Datasets_Final Table ([Dataset]
Nvarchar(Max), [Parameter] Nvarchar(Max))

Insert Into @Raw_Datasets_Final ([Dataset],
[Parameter])

Select

        (Case When
CharIndex(@CSV_Column_Delimiter, [Value], 0)
= 0 Then Null Else Replace(Left([Value],
(Len([Value]) -
CharIndex(@CSV_Column_Delimiter,
Reverse([Value]), 0))), Char(10), '') End) As
[Dataset],

        (Case When
CharIndex(@CSV_Column_Delimiter, [Value], 0)
= 0 Then Null Else Replace(Right([Value],
CharIndex(@CSV_Column_Delimiter,
Reverse([Value]), 0)), @CSV_Column_Delimiter,
'') End) As [Parameter]

From @Raw_Datasets_Intermediate

Where
```

```
        (Case When
CharIndex(@CSV_Column_Delimiter, [Value], 0)
= 0 Then Null Else Replace(Left([Value],
(Len([Value]) -
CharIndex(@CSV_Column_Delimiter,
Reverse([Value]), 0))), Char(10), '') End) <>
'Dataset'

        And (Case When
CharIndex(@CSV_Column_Delimiter, [Value], 0)
= 0 Then Null Else Replace(Left([Value],
(Len([Value]) -
CharIndex(@CSV_Column_Delimiter,
Reverse([Value]), 0))), Char(10), '') End) <>
'Parameter'

        And [Value] <> Char(10)



--The following codeblock aggregates the
datasets into multiple rows, which correspond
to the parameter count transformation

Declare @Dataset_Parameter_Counts Table
([Dataset] Nvarchar(Max), [Parameter_Count]
BigInt)

Insert Into @Dataset_Parameter_Counts
([Dataset], [Parameter_Count])
```

```
Select

        [Dataset] As [Dataset],

        Count(*) As [Parameter_Count]

From @Raw_Datasets_Final

Group By [Dataset]
```

--The following codeblock assigns an analysis label, which must be used later on in the query alongside a datetime stamp, in order to generate a unique ID

```
Declare @Analysis_Label Nvarchar(Max)

Set @Analysis_Label = (Select
String_Agg([Dataset], '_') Within Group (Order
By [Dataset] Asc) From
@Dataset_Parameter_Counts)
```

--VALIDATION STAGE PART ONE

Select (@Analysis_Label + ':Validation Stage Part One Started At Around:' + Cast(GetDate() As Nvarchar(Max))) As [Execution_Progress]

--The following codeblocks, perform data input validation checks, to reduce later algorithm errors, and terminates the current query instance if a check fails... otherwise the query proceeds to analyse Michaelian probabilities... There is one more validation check separated to later on in the query, because the sampling technique augments the input data to remove outliers.

Declare @Validation_Checks_Table_Variable Table ([Check] TinyInt)

Insert Into @Validation_Checks_Table_Variable ([Check])

Values ((Case When @Exploding_Probability_Gradient_Dataset_Range_Limit_Percentage <= 80 Then (Case When @Exploding_Probability_Gradient_Dataset_Range_Limit_Percentage > 0 Then Null Else 1 End) Else 1 End)) --Check for @Exploding_Probability_Gradient_Dataset_Ran ge_Limit_Percentage global variable inside of allowed range of values.

```
Insert Into @Validation_Checks_Table_Variable
([Check])

Select

        Avg(2) As [Check]

From
@Dynamic_SQL_Intermediate_Table_Variable_
1

Where Left([Data], 19) <> ('Dataset,Parameter'
+ Char(13) + Char(10)) --Check for two correctly
named and correctly column delimited columns
error.

Union All

Select

        Avg(3) As [Check]

From @Raw_Datasets_Intermediate

Where

        [Value] <> Char(10)

        And
CharIndex(@CSV_Column_Delimiter, [Value], 0)
```

= 0 --Check for presence of the designated column Delimiter on each row error.

Union All

Select

Avg(4) As [Check]

From @Raw_Datasets_Intermediate

Where

[Value] <> Char(10)

And Len(Replace([Value], @CSV_Column_Delimiter, '')) <> (Len([Value]) - 1) --Check for no dataset value or parameter value extra column Delimiters error.

Union All

Select

Avg(5) As [Check]

From @Raw_Datasets_Final

Where [Dataset] Is Null Or [Parameter] Is Null Or [Dataset] = '' Or [Parameter] = '' --Check for no null or empty values in either column error.

Union All

Select

```
        Avg(6) As [Check]

From @Raw_Datasets_Final A

Left Join @Raw_Datasets_Final B

        On (B.[Dataset] = A.[Dataset] And
B.[Parameter] <> A.[Parameter])

Left Join @Raw_Datasets_Final C

        On (C.[Dataset] = A.[Dataset] And
C.[Parameter] <> A.[Parameter] And
C.[Parameter] <> B.[Parameter])

Where C.[Dataset] Is Null --Check for essential
distribution with more than 3 unique parameter
values error.

Union All

Select

        Avg(7) As [Check]

From @Raw_Datasets_Final

Where IsNumeric([Dataset]) = 1 Or
IsNumeric([Parameter]) = 0 --Check for correct
data type in either column error (Dataset
column should be Text, Parameter column
should be Numeric).

Union All
```

```
Select

        Avg(8) As [Check]

From @Raw_Datasets_Final

Where Len([Dataset]) > 250 --Check for dataset
labels having less than or equal to 250
characters.

Union All

Select 0 As [Check] --This is so that there is no
null variable behaviour, which can lead to
obscure bugs later on.


Declare @Data_Validation_Checks_Max TinyInt

Set @Data_Validation_Checks_Max = (Select
Max([Check]) From
@Validation_Checks_Table_Variable)


--(Global Variable Checks)

If (Select Min([Check]) From
@Validation_Checks_Table_Variable Where
[Check] = 1) = 1

Select 'Global variable check for
@Exploding_Probability_Gradient_Dataset_Ran
ge_Limit_Percentage global variable inside of
```

allowed range of values failed. Please make sure you have set this variable, which is near the start of the source code of this query, to a value which is between 0% (not inclusive) and 80% (inclusive).' As [Data_Input_Error]

--(Metadata Checks)

If (Select Min([Check]) From @Validation_Checks_Table_Variable Where [Check] = 2) = 2

Select 'Input/Source CSV metadata check for two correctly named and correctly column delimited columns failed. Please make sure you have not changed or deleted the original column headers from the Datasets_For_Michaelian_Probability_Analysis. csv template. You may also need to check for invisible extra spaces.' As [Data_Input_Error]

If (Select Min([Check]) From @Validation_Checks_Table_Variable Where [Check] = 3 Or [Check] = 1 Or [Check] = 2) = 3 -- Nominal check (Or [Check] = 1 Or [Check] = 2) for colliding validation effects (One data validation error, can inadvertently cause multiple validation errors which were not in the source data.)

Select 'Input/Source CSV metadata check for presence of the designated column Delimiter on each row error. The designated CSV file column Delimiter is assigned in the global variables near the beginning of the source code of this query. Alternatively, you could change the CSV column delimiter in your input file, but this would likely involve more effort.' As [Data_Input_Error]

If (Select Min([Check]) From @Validation_Checks_Table_Variable Where [Check] = 4 Or [Check] = 1 Or [Check] = 2 Or [Check] = 3) = 4 --Nominal check (Or [Check] = 1 Or [Check] = 2 Or [Check] = 3) for colliding validation effects (One data validation error, can inadvertently cause multiple validation errors which were not in the source data.)

Select 'Input/Source CSV metadata check for no dataset value or parameter value extra column Delimiters failed. This algorithm does not allow column Delimiters in either the dataset or parameter column values.' As [Data_Input_Error]

--(Data Checks)

If (Select Min([Check]) From @Validation_Checks_Table_Variable Where [Check] = 5 Or [Check] = 1 Or [Check] = 2 Or [Check] = 3 Or [Check] = 4) = 5 --Nominal check (Or [Check] = 1 Or [Check] = 2 Or [Check] = 3 Or [Check] = 4) for colliding validation effects (One data validation error, can inadvertently cause multiple validation errors which were not in the source data.)

Select 'Input/Source CSV data check for no null or empty values in either column failed.' As [Data_Input_Error]

If (Select Min([Check]) From @Validation_Checks_Table_Variable Where [Check] = 6 Or [Check] = 1 Or [Check] = 2 Or [Check] = 3 Or [Check] = 4) = 6 --Nominal check (Or [Check] = 1 Or [Check] = 2 Or [Check] = 3 Or [Check] = 4) for colliding validation effects (One data validation error, can inadvertently cause multiple validation errors which were not in the source data.)

Select 'Input/Source CSV data check for essential distribution with more than 3 unique parameter values per dataset failed.' As [Data_Input_Error]

If (Select Min([Check]) From @Validation_Checks_Table_Variable Where [Check] = 7 Or [Check] = 1 Or [Check] = 2 Or [Check] = 3 Or [Check] = 4) = 7 --Nominal check (Or [Check] = 1 Or [Check] = 2 Or [Check] = 3 Or [Check] = 4) for colliding validation effects (One data validation error, can inadvertently cause multiple validation errors which were not in the source data.)

Select 'Input/Source CSV data check for correct data type in either column failed (Dataset column should be Text, Parameter column should be Numeric).' As [Data_Input_Error]

If (Select Min([Check]) From @Validation_Checks_Table_Variable Where [Check] = 8 Or [Check] = 1 Or [Check] = 2 Or [Check] = 3 Or [Check] = 4) = 8 --Nominal check (Or [Check] = 1 Or [Check] = 2 Or [Check] = 3 Or [Check] = 4) for colliding validation effects (One data validation error, can inadvertently cause multiple validation errors which were not in the source data.)

Select 'Input/Source CSV data check for dataset labels having less than or equal to 250 characters.' As [Data_Input_Error]

--Execution Termination

If @Data_Validation_Checks_Max > 0

Set NoExec On

--Execution Progression

If @Data_Validation_Checks_Max = 0

Select (@Analysis_Label + ':Sampling Stage
Started At Around:' + Cast(GetDate() As
Nvarchar(Max))) As [Execution_Progress]

--SAMPLING STAGE:

--You can remove the sampling stage altogether
where appropriate (in most cases), and
experience a significant query speed boost. This
approach is called bootstrapping, and should be
almost mandatory seeing as future algorithms
will likely need to over-whelmingly be of the
real-time kind!

--The core of the deepset partitioning algorithm
involves an initial unique dataset-parameter
sampling round, which is followed by an
additive impartial dataset-parameter sampling
round, if more samples are still needed. In both
cases, we use what I call the Round-Rand-Robin
sampling technique, which utilises a loop that

keeps reassigning triple-compound rand values to remaining parameters until every parameter in a given dataset has a unique triple-compound rand value. This random ordering of parameters in a dataset can then be used in order to sample to a given degree of statistical significance, as required by the user (global variable).

--The following codeblock simply corrects column data types.

Declare @Data_Type_Corrected_Datasets Table ([Dataset] Nvarchar(250), [Parameter] Float)

Insert Into @Data_Type_Corrected_Datasets ([Dataset], [Parameter])

Select

[Dataset] As [Dataset],

Cast([Parameter] As Float) As [Parameter]

From @Raw_Datasets_Final

--The following codeblock loads the raw datasets into a table variable, which corresponds to the dataset range transformation

```
Declare @Dataset_Ranges Table ([Dataset]
Nvarchar(250), [Range] Float)

Insert Into @Dataset_Ranges ([Dataset],
[Range])

Select

        [Dataset] As [Dataset],

        (Max([Parameter]) - Min([Parameter]))
As [Range]

From @Data_Type_Corrected_Datasets

Group By [Dataset]
```

```
--The following codeblock allows us to later
remove outliers from the dataset observations.

Declare @Datasets_Outlier_Augmented Table
([Dataset] Nvarchar(250), [Parameter] Float,
[Outlier_Threshold_Count] BigInt)

Insert Into @Datasets_Outlier_Augmented
([Dataset], [Parameter],
[Outlier_Threshold_Count])

Select

        A.[Dataset] As [Dataset],
```

```
        A.[Parameter] As [Parameter],

        Count(*) As [Outlier_Threshold_Count]

From @Data_Type_Corrected_Datasets A

Inner Join @Dataset_Ranges B

        On (B.[Dataset] = A.[Dataset])

Inner Join @Raw_Datasets_Final C

        On (C.[Dataset] = A.[Dataset] And
C.[Parameter] >= (A.[Parameter] - (B.[Range] *
(@Outlier_Threshold_Percentage / 100))) And
C.[Parameter] <= (A.[Parameter] + (B.[Range] *
(@Outlier_Threshold_Percentage / 100))))

Group By A.[Dataset], A.[Parameter]
```

--The following codeblock adds an order column to the deepsets in order to maintain uniqueness later on

```
Declare @Deepset_Partitions_Intermediate
Table ([Unique_Order] BigInt, [Dataset]
Nvarchar(250), [Parameter] Float)

Insert Into @Deepset_Partitions_Intermediate
([Unique_Order], [Dataset], [Parameter])
```

```
Select

        Row_Number() Over(Order By (Select
Null) Asc) As [Unique_Order],

        A.[Dataset] As [Dataset],

        A.[Parameter] As [Parameter]

From @Data_Type_Corrected_Datasets A

Inner Join @Datasets_Outlier_Augmented B

        On (B.[Dataset] = A.[Dataset] And
B.[Parameter] = A.[Parameter] And
B.[Outlier_Threshold_Count] > 2) --You could
turn the second term after the operator here
into another global variable... but, for me, I
follow Jesus Christ, and the bible clearly states
that 3 witnesses are sufficient to prove any
claim.
```

```
--The following codeblock produces initial
unique parameter pool

Declare
@Deepset_Partitions_Initial_Unique_Sampling_
Round_Parameter_Pool  Table ([Unique_Order]
BigInt, [Dataset] Nvarchar(250), [Parameter]
Float)
```

```
Insert Into
@Deepset_Partitions_Initial_Unique_Sampling_
Round_Parameter_Pool ([Unique_Order],
[Dataset], [Parameter])

Select

        Min([Unique_Order]) As
[Unique_Order],

        [Dataset] As [Dataset],

        [Parameter] As [Parameter]

From @Deepset_Partitions_Intermediate

Group By [Dataset], [Parameter] --The minimum
unique order grouping allows us to perform a
unique first round-rand-robin sampling
technique, before later on, simply randomly
sampling each dataset's parameters. This initial
unique sampling round is necessary, in order to
maintain essential dataset distribution (at least
3 unique parameters).




--The following codeblock produces the additive
impartial parameter pool

Declare
@Deepset_Partitions_Additive_Impartial_Samp
```

```
ling_Round_Parameter_Pool  Table
([Unique_Order] BigInt, [Dataset]
Nvarchar(250), [Parameter] Float)

Insert Into
@Deepset_Partitions_Additive_Impartial_Samp
ling_Round_Parameter_Pool ([Unique_Order],
[Dataset], [Parameter])

Select

        A.[Unique_Order] As [Unique_Order],

        A.[Dataset] As [Dataset],

        A.[Parameter] As [Parameter]

From @Deepset_Partitions_Intermediate A

Left Outer Join
@Deepset_Partitions_Initial_Unique_Sampling_
Round_Parameter_Pool B

        On (B.[Unique_Order] =
A.[Unique_Order]) --This join excludes already
partitioned parameters handled within the
initial unique sampling round.

Where B.[Unique_Order] Is Null
```

--The following codeblocks split individual observations into multiple different deepset partitions (optimal sample groups).

--(((Initial Unique Sampling Round)))

Declare @Deepset_Partitions_Intermediate_Initial_Unique_Round_A Table ([Unique_Order] BigInt, [Dataset] Nvarchar(250), [Rand_1] Float, [Rand_2] Float, [Rand_3] Float)

Declare @Deepset_Partitions_Intermediate_Initial_Unique_Round_B Table ([Dataset] Nvarchar(250), [Rand_1] Float, [Rand_2] Float, [Rand_3] Float, [Count] BigInt)

Declare @Loop_Count BigInt

Set @Loop_Count = 0

--(In this loop below, in order to maintain sampling symmetry we make sure that each dataset-parameter pairing has its own unique triple-compound rand value... Otherwise, in some cases (where there are multiple different parameter values with the same [Rand] value) the row ordering would favour the lower parameter value over the greater parameter value, or vice-versa.)

While (Case When Exists(Select (1) From @Deepset_Partitions_Intermediate_Initial_Unique_Round_B Where [Count] > 1) Then (Case When @Loop_Count < 1000 Then 1 Else 0 End) Else (Case When @Loop_Count = 0 Then 1 Else 0 End) End) > 0 --Option (Maxrecursion 1000)... Limited sampling rounds for loop safety reasons... You may want to increase this, if you have hyper-scale datasets of more than a billion parameters per dataset... Please handle exceptions yourself (when the max recursion limit is breached!)... !!!!!BUT!!!!! it would be far preferable in computational terms for you to simply add more rand columns to the round-rand-robin technique instead.

Begin

      Set @Loop_Count = (@Loop_Count + 1)

      Delete From @Deepset_Partitions_Intermediate_Initial_Unique_Round_A

      Insert Into @Deepset_Partitions_Intermediate_Initial_Unique_Round_A ([Unique_Order], [Dataset], [Rand_1], [Rand_2], [Rand_3])

```
Select

        [Unique_Order] As
[Unique_Order],

        [Dataset] As [Dataset],

        Rand(CheckSum(NewID())) As
[Rand_1],

        Rand(CheckSum(NewID())) As
[Rand_2],

        Rand(CheckSum(NewID())) As
[Rand_3]

    From
@Deepset_Partitions_Initial_Unique_Sampling_
Round_Parameter_Pool


    Delete From
@Deepset_Partitions_Intermediate_Initial_Uni
que_Round_B

    Insert Into
@Deepset_Partitions_Intermediate_Initial_Uni
que_Round_B ([Dataset], [Rand_1], [Rand_2],
[Rand_3], [Count])

    Select

        [Dataset] As [Dataset],
```

```
        [Rand_1] As [Rand_1],

        [Rand_2] As [Rand_2],

        [Rand_3] As [Rand_3],

        Count(*) As [Count]

    From
@Deepset_Partitions_Intermediate_Initial_Uni
que_Round_A

    Group By [Dataset], [Rand_1], [Rand_2],
[Rand_3]

    --Eventually the loop will work through
all dataset-round-rand-robin duplicates until all
triple-compound rand values are unique.



End



Declare
@Deepset_Partitions_Intermediate_Initial_Uni
que_Round_C Table ([Unique_Order] BigInt,
[Dataset] Nvarchar(250), [Parameter] Float,
[Rand_1] Float, [Rand_2] Float, [Rand_3] Float,
[Initial_Order] BigInt)

Insert Into
@Deepset_Partitions_Intermediate_Initial_Uni
```

que_Round_C ([Unique_Order], [Dataset], [Parameter], [Rand_1], [Rand_2], [Rand_3], [Initial_Order])

Select

A.[Unique_Order] As [Unique_Order],

B.[Dataset] As [Dataset],

B.[Parameter] As [Parameter],

A.[Rand_1] As [Rand_1],

A.[Rand_2] As [Rand_2],

A.[Rand_3] As [Rand_3],

Row_Number() Over(Partition By B.[Dataset] Order By A.[Rand_1] Asc, A.[Rand_2] Asc, A.[Rand_3] Asc) As [Initial_Order]

From @Deepset_Partitions_Intermediate_Initial_Unique_Round_A A

Inner Join @Deepset_Partitions_Intermediate B

On (B.[Unique_Order] = A.[Unique_Order])

```
Declare @Deepset_Partitions_Final Table
([Deepset_Partition] Nvarchar(250),
[Unique_Order] BigInt, [Dataset] Nvarchar(250),
[Parameter] Float)

Insert Into @Deepset_Partitions_Final
([Deepset_Partition], [Unique_Order],
[Dataset], [Parameter])

Select

        (Case When [Initial_Order] <=
Ceiling((100 /
@Target_Deepset_Training_Significance)) Then
'1-Training' Else '2-Other' End) As
[Deepset_Partition], --Ceiling(), because you
want at least the target significance... You could
add other partitions here, as desired, using the
same technique.... and even maybe route the
partitions off to different parallel models and/or
compute engines.

        [Unique_Order] As [Unique_Order],

        [Dataset] As [Dataset],

        [Parameter] As [Parameter]

From
@Deepset_Partitions_Intermediate_Initial_Uni
que_Round_C
```

```
Declare
@Deepset_Initial_Unique_Sampling_Round_Co
unts Table ([Dataset] Nvarchar(250),
[Sample_Count] BigInt)

Insert Into
@Deepset_Initial_Unique_Sampling_Round_Co
unts ([Dataset], [Sample_Count])

Select

        [Dataset] As [Dataset],

        Count(*) As [Sample_Count]

From @Deepset_Partitions_Final

Where [Deepset_Partition] = '1-Training'

Group By [Dataset]


--(((Additive Impartial Sampling Round)))

Declare
@Deepset_Partitions_Intermediate_Additive_I
mpartial_Round_A Table ([Unique_Order]
BigInt, [Dataset] Nvarchar(250), [Rand_1] Float,
[Rand_2] Float, [Rand_3] Float)

Declare
@Deepset_Partitions_Intermediate_Additive_I
mpartial_Round_B Table ([Dataset]
```

Nvarchar(250), [Rand_1] Float, [Rand_2] Float, [Rand_3] Float, [Count] BigInt)

Set @Loop_Count = 0

--(In this loop below, in order to maintain sampling symmetry we make sure that each dataset-parameter pairing has its own unique triple-compound rand value... Otherwise, in some cases (where there are multiple different parameter values with the same [Rand] value) the row ordering would favour the lower parameter value over the greater parameter value, or vice-versa.)

While (Case When Exists(Select (1) From @Deepset_Partitions_Intermediate_Additive_Impartial_Round_B Where [Count] > 1) Then (Case When @Loop_Count < 1000 Then 1 Else 0 End) Else (Case When @Loop_Count = 0 Then 1 Else 0 End) End) > 0 --Option (Maxrecursion 1000)... Limited sampling rounds for loop safety reasons... You may want to increase this, if you have hyper-scale datasets of more than a billion parameters per dataset... Please handle exceptions yourself (when the max recursion limit is breached!)... !!!!!BUT!!!!! it would be far preferable in computational terms for you to simply add more rand columns to the round-rand-robin technique instead.

Begin

```
Set @Loop_Count = (@Loop_Count + 1)



Delete From
@Deepset_Partitions_Intermediate_Additive_I
mpartial_Round_A

Insert Into
@Deepset_Partitions_Intermediate_Additive_I
mpartial_Round_A ([Unique_Order], [Dataset],
[Rand_1], [Rand_2], [Rand_3])

Select

        [Unique_Order] As
[Unique_Order],

        [Dataset] As [Dataset],

        Rand(CheckSum(NewID())) As
[Rand_1],

        Rand(CheckSum(NewID())) As
[Rand_2],

        Rand(CheckSum(NewID())) As
[Rand_3]
```

From
@Deepset_Partitions_Additive_Impartial_Samp
ling_Round_Parameter_Pool

Delete From
@Deepset_Partitions_Intermediate_Additive_I
mpartial_Round_B

Insert Into
@Deepset_Partitions_Intermediate_Additive_I
mpartial_Round_B ([Dataset], [Rand_1],
[Rand_2], [Rand_3], [Count])

Select

[Dataset] As [Dataset],

[Rand_1] As [Rand_1],

[Rand_2] As [Rand_2],

[Rand_3] As [Rand_3],

Count(*) As [Count]

From
@Deepset_Partitions_Intermediate_Additive_I
mpartial_Round_A

Group By [Dataset], [Rand_1], [Rand_2],
[Rand_3]

--Eventually the loop will work through all dataset-round-rand-robin duplicates until all triple-compound rand values are unique.

End

Declare @Deepset_Partitions_Intermediate_Additive_Impartial_Round_C Table ([Unique_Order] BigInt, [Dataset] Nvarchar(250), [Parameter] Float, [Rand_1] Float, [Rand_2] Float, [Rand_3] Float, [Additive_Order] BigInt)

Insert Into @Deepset_Partitions_Intermediate_Additive_Impartial_Round_C ([Unique_Order], [Dataset], [Parameter], [Rand_1], [Rand_2], [Rand_3], [Additive_Order])

Select

A.[Unique_Order] As [Unique_Order],

B.[Dataset] As [Dataset],

B.[Parameter] As [Parameter],

A.[Rand_1] As [Rand_1],

A.[Rand_2] As [Rand_2],

```
        A.[Rand_3] As [Rand_3],

        Row_Number() Over(Partition By
B.[Dataset] Order By A.[Rand_1] Asc,
A.[Rand_2] Asc, A.[Rand_3] Asc) As
[Additive_Order]

From
@Deepset_Partitions_Intermediate_Additive_I
mpartial_Round_A A

Inner Join @Deepset_Partitions_Intermediate B

        On (B.[Unique_Order] =
A.[Unique_Order])


Insert Into @Deepset_Partitions_Final
([Deepset_Partition], [Unique_Order],
[Dataset], [Parameter])

Select

        (Case When A.[Additive_Order] <=
(Ceiling((100 /
@Target_Deepset_Training_Significance)) -
B.[Sample_Count]) Then '1-Training' Else '2-
Other' End) As [Deepset_Partition], --Ceiling(),
because you want at least the target
significance... You could add other partitions
here, as desired, using the same technique....
```

and even maybe route the partitions off to different parallel models or compute engines.

    A.[Unique_Order] As [Unique_Order],

    A.[Dataset] As [Dataset],

    A.[Parameter] As [Parameter]

From @Deepset_Partitions_Intermediate_Additive_Impartial_Round_C A

Inner Join @Deepset_Initial_Unique_Sampling_Round_Counts B --This join is used in the [Deepset_Partition] column, in order to correct augment the @Target_Deepset_Training_Significance variable method for limiting training sample rows.

    On (B.[Dataset] = A.[Dataset])

--The following codeblocks transform the deepsets into statistical significance sigma-bands for all datasets

Declare @Deepset_Statistical_Significance_Sigma_Band

s Table ([Dataset] Nvarchar(250),
[Post_Sampling_Sigma_Band] Nvarchar(250))

Insert Into
@Deepset_Statistical_Significance_Sigma_Band
s ([Dataset], [Post_Sampling_Sigma_Band])

Select

[Dataset] As [Dataset],

(Case When Count(*) < 100 Then
'Loose' Else (Case When Count(*) < 1000 Then
'Lean' Else (Case When Count(*) < 10000 Then
'1-Sigma' Else (Case When Count(*) < 100000
Then '2-Sigma' Else (Case When Count(*) <
1000000 Then '3-Sigma' Else (Case When
Count(*) < 10000000 Then '4-Sigma' Else (Case
When Count(*) < 100000000 Then '5-Sigma'
Else (Case When Count(*) < 1000000000 Then
'6-Sigma' Else 'Statistically Unnecessary
Significance' End) End) End) End) End) End) End)
End) As [Post_Sampling_Sigma_Band]

From @Deepset_Partitions_Final

Where [Deepset_Partition] = '1-Training'

Group By [Dataset]

```
Insert Into
@Deepset_Statistical_Significance_Sigma_Band
s ([Dataset], [Post_Sampling_Sigma_Band])

Select

        A.[Dataset] As [Dataset],

        'Every Parameter Is An Outlier' As
[Post_Sampling_Sigma_Band] --Sometimes a
dataset will be totally excluded from analysis,
because all of its parameters have been
classified as outliers.

From @Dataset_Parameter_Counts A

Left Outer Join
@Deepset_Statistical_Significance_Sigma_Band
s B

        On (B.[Dataset] = A.[Dataset])

Where B.[Dataset] Is Null
```

```
--The following codeblock loads the deepsets
into an ordered deepset table variable

Declare @Deepsets Table ([Order] BigInt,
[Deepset_Partition] Nvarchar(250), [Dataset]
Nvarchar(250), [Parameter] Float)
```

```
Insert Into @Deepsets ([Order],
[Deepset_Partition], [Dataset], [Parameter])

Select

        Row_Number() Over(Order By (Select
Null) Asc) As [Order],

        [Deepset_Partition] As
[Deepset_Partition],

        [Dataset] As [Dataset],

        [Parameter] As [Parameter]

From @Deepset_Partitions_Final




--LOAD STAGE PART ONE:

Select (@Analysis_Label + ':Load Stage Part One
Started At Around:' + Cast(GetDate() As
Nvarchar(Max))) As [Execution_Progress]
```

--The following codeblock returns all current useful data of interest from this algorithm

```
Select * From
@Deepset_Statistical_Significance_Sigma_Band
s Order By [Dataset] Asc,
[Post_Sampling_Sigma_Band] Asc
```

--VALIDATION STAGE PART TWO

```
Select (@Analysis_Label + ':Validation Stage
Part Two Started At Around:' + Cast(GetDate()
As Nvarchar(Max))) As [Execution_Progress]
```

--The following codeblocks, continue data input validation checks, to reduce later algorithm errors, and terminates the current query instance if a check fails... otherwise the query proceeds to analyse Michaelian probabilities... This is the extra validation check separated to later on in the query, because the sampling technique augments the input data to remove outliers.

Insert Into @Validation_Checks_Table_Variable ([Check])

Select

Avg(9) As [Check]

From @Deepsets A

Left Join @Deepsets B

On (B.[Dataset] = A.[Dataset] And B.[Parameter] <> A.[Parameter])

Left Join @Deepsets C

On (C.[Dataset] = A.[Dataset] And C.[Parameter] <> A.[Parameter] And C.[Parameter] <> B.[Parameter])

Where C.[Dataset] Is Null --Check for essential distribution with more than 3 unique parameter values error.

Set @Data_Validation_Checks_Max = (Select Max([Check]) From @Validation_Checks_Table_Variable)

--(Data Checks)

If (Select Min([Check]) From
@Validation_Checks_Table_Variable Where
[Check] = 9 Or [Check] = 1 Or [Check] = 2 Or
[Check] = 3 Or [Check] = 4) = 9 --Nominal check (
Or [Check] = 1 Or [Check] = 2 Or [Check] = 3 Or
[Check] = 4) for colliding validation effects (One
data validation error, can inadvertently cause
multiple validation errors which were not in the
source data.)

Select 'Sampled deepset data check for
essential distribution with more than 3 unique
parameter values per dataset failed... It could
be that some parameters have been removed
by the sampling stage because they were
classified as outliers. If so, please either omit
the appropriate dataset, which can be found in
the
@Deepset_Statistical_Significance_Sigma_Band
s table variable, or, if appropriate for your
analytical requirements, please amend the
global variable near the start of the source code
of this query, called
@Outlier_Threshold_Percentage.' As
[Data_Input_Error]

--Execution Termination

If @Data_Validation_Checks_Max > 0

Set NoExec On

--Execution Progression

If @Data_Validation_Checks_Max = 0

Select (@Analysis_Label + ':Transformation Stage Started At Around:' + Cast(GetDate() As Nvarchar(Max))) As [Execution_Progress]

--TRANSFORMATION STAGE:

--The following codeblock loads the parameter count transformation into a variable, which corresponds to the minimum cross-normalisation row count transformation

Declare @Minimum_Deepset_Parameter_Count BigInt

```
Set @Minimum_Deepset_Parameter_Count =
(Select Min([Parameter_Count]) From
@Dataset_Parameter_Counts)
```

```
--The following codeblock loads the deepsets
into a table variable, which corresponds to the
cross-normalisation transformation
```

```
Declare @Deepset_Cross_Normalisations Table
([Order] BigInt, [Dataset] Nvarchar(250),
[Cross_Normalised_Parameter] Float)
```

```
Insert Into @Deepset_Cross_Normalisations
([Order], [Dataset],
[Cross_Normalised_Parameter])
```

```
Select

        A.[Order] As [Order],

        A.[Dataset] As [Dataset],

        Sum((((A.[Parameter] *
C.[Parameter_Count]) / B.[Parameter_Count]) /
@Minimum_Deepset_Parameter_Count) *
B.[Parameter_Count]) As
[Cross_Normalised_Parameter]
```

```
From @Deepsets A
```

Inner Join @Dataset_Parameter_Counts B

On (B.[Dataset] = A.[Dataset] And A.[Deepset_Partition] = '1-Training')

Inner Join @Dataset_Parameter_Counts C

On (C.[Dataset] <> A.[Dataset] And A.[Deepset_Partition] = '1-Training')

Group By A.[Dataset], A.[Order]

--To cross-normalise a dataset significance, you need to: (((multiply the current dataset significance by the sum of all other dataset parameter counts), divide by the sum of the current dataset parameter count), and finally divide by the minimum dataset parameter count).

--The following codeblock loads the cross-normalisation deepsets into a table variable, which corresponds to the cross-normalisation range transformation

Declare @Deepset_Cross_Normalisation_Ranges Table ([Dataset] Nvarchar(250), [Range] Float)

```
Insert Into
@Deepset_Cross_Normalisation_Ranges
([Dataset], [Range])

Select

        [Dataset] As [Dataset],

        (Max([Cross_Normalised_Parameter]) -
Min([Cross_Normalised_Parameter])) As
[Range]

From @Deepset_Cross_Normalisations

Group By [Dataset]
```

```
--The following codeblocks loads the cross-
normalisation range transformation into a
variable, which corresponds to the maximum
cross-normalisation range transformation

Declare
@Deepset_Cross_Normalisation_Maximum_Ra
nge Float

Set
@Deepset_Cross_Normalisation_Maximum_Ra
nge = (Select Max([Range]) From
@Deepset_Cross_Normalisation_Ranges)
```

--The following codeblock loads the cross-normalised deepsets into a table variable, which corresponds to the proportional-normalisation transformation

Declare @Deepset_Proportional_Normalisations Table ([Order] BigInt, [Dataset] Nvarchar(250), [Proportional_Normalised_Parameter] Float)

Insert Into @Deepset_Proportional_Normalisations ([Order], [Dataset], [Proportional_Normalised_Parameter])

Select

       A.[Order] As [Order],

       A.[Dataset] As [Dataset],

       (A.[Cross_Normalised_Parameter] / (B.[Range] / @Deepset_Cross_Normalisation_Maximum_Range)) As [Proportional_Normalised_Parameter]

From @Deepset_Cross_Normalisations A

Inner Join @Deepset_Cross_Normalisation_Ranges B

On (B.[Dataset] = A.[Dataset])

--The following codeblock loads the proportional-normalisation tranformation into a table variable, which corresponds to the proportional-normalisation deepset minimum parameter transformation

Declare @Deepset_Proportional_Normalisation_Param eter_Minimum Table ([Dataset] Nvarchar(250), [Proportional_Parameter_Minimum] Float)

Insert Into @Deepset_Proportional_Normalisation_Param eter_Minimum ([Dataset], [Proportional_Parameter_Minimum])

Select

[Dataset] As [Dataset],

Min([Proportional_Normalised_Parame ter]) As [Proportional_Parameter_Minimum]

From @Deepset_Proportional_Normalisations

Group By [Dataset]

--The following codeblock loads the proportional-normalised transformation into a table variable, which corresponds to the scale-normalisation transformation

```
Declare @Deepset_Scale_Normalisations Table
([Order] BigInt, [Dataset] Nvarchar(250),
[Scale_Normalised_Parameter] Float)

Insert Into @Deepset_Scale_Normalisations
([Order], [Dataset],
[Scale_Normalised_Parameter])

Select

        A.[Order] As [Order],

        A.[Dataset] As [Dataset],

        (A.[Proportional_Normalised_Paramete
r] - B.[Proportional_Parameter_Minimum]) As
[Scale_Normalised_Parameter]

From @Deepset_Proportional_Normalisations
A

Inner Join
@Deepset_Proportional_Normalisation_Param
eter_Minimum B

        On (B.[Dataset] = A.[Dataset])
```

--The following codeblock loads the scale-normalisation transformation into a variable, which corresponds to the scale-normalisation maximum parameter transformation

```
Declare
@Scale_Normalisation_Maximum_Parameter
Float
```

```
Set
@Scale_Normalisation_Maximum_Parameter =
(Select Max([Scale_Normalised_Parameter])
From @Deepset_Scale_Normalisations)
```

--The following codeblock loads the deepsets into a table variable, which corresponds to the fully normalised parameter transformation

```
Declare @Fully_Normalised_Deepsets Table
([Order] BigInt, [Dataset] Nvarchar(250),
[Fully_Normalised_Parameter] Float)
```

```
Insert Into @Fully_Normalised_Deepsets
([Order], [Dataset],
[Fully_Normalised_Parameter])
```

```
Select

        [Order] As [Order],

        [Dataset] As [Dataset],

        ((([Scale_Normalised_Parameter] /
@Scale_Normalisation_Maximum_Parameter)
* 100) As [Fully_Normalised_Parameter]

From @Deepset_Scale_Normalisations
```

--The following codeblock finds the fully normalised deepset parameter minimas

--Declare @Deepset_Fully_Normalised_Parameter_Minimum Float (You could fudge this transformation for a slight speed gain under some circumstances, but would need to tweak following source code references.)

--Set @Deepset_Fully_Normalised_Parameter_Minimum = 0 (You could fudge this transformation for a slight speed gain under some circumstances, but would need to tweak following source code references.)

--The following codeblock aggregates the deepsets into multiple rows, which correspond to the fully normalised deepset parameter minimum transformation

```
Declare
@Deepset_Fully_Normalised_Parameter_Mini
mas Table ([Dataset] Nvarchar(250),
[Parameter_Minimum] Float)

Insert Into
@Deepset_Fully_Normalised_Parameter_Mini
mas ([Dataset], [Parameter_Minimum])

Select

        [Dataset] As [Dataset],

        Min([Fully_Normalised_Parameter]) As
[Parameter_Minimum]

From @Fully_Normalised_Deepsets

Group By [Dataset]
```

--The following codeblock finds the fully normalised deepset parameter maximas

```
--Declare
@Deepset_Fully_Normalised_Parameter_Maxi
```

mum Float (You could fudge this transformation for a slight speed gain under some circumstances, but would need to tweak following source code references.)

--Set @Deepset_Fully_Normalised_Parameter_Maximum = 100 (You could fudge this transformation for a slight speed gain under some circumstances, but would need to tweak following source code references.)

--The following codeblock aggregates the deepsets into multiple rows, which correspond to the fully normalised deepset parameter maximum transformation

Declare @Deepset_Fully_Normalised_Parameter_Maximas Table ([Dataset] Nvarchar(250), [Parameter_Maximum] Float)

Insert Into @Deepset_Fully_Normalised_Parameter_Maximas ([Dataset], [Parameter_Maximum])

Select

    [Dataset] As [Dataset],

    Max([Fully_Normalised_Parameter]) As [Parameter_Maximum]

From @Fully_Normalised_Deepsets

Group By [Dataset]

--The following codeblock finds the fully normalised dataset parameter ranges

--Declare @Deepset_Fully_Normalised_Parameter_Range Float (You could fudge this transformation for a slight speed gain under some circumstances, but would need to tweak following source code references.)

--Set @Deepset_Fully_Normalised_Parameter_Range = 100 (You could fudge this transformation for a slight speed gain under some circumstances, but would need to tweak following source code references.)

--The following codeblock aggregates the deepsets into multiple rows, which correspond to the fully normalised deepset parameter range transformation

Declare @Deepset_Fully_Normalised_Parameter_Range

```
s Table ([Dataset] Nvarchar(250),
[Parameter_Range] Float)

Insert Into
@Deepset_Fully_Normalised_Parameter_Range
s ([Dataset], [Parameter_Range])

Select

        A.[Dataset] As [Dataset],

        Avg(B.[Parameter_Maximum] -
A.[Parameter_Minimum]) As
[Parameter_Range]

From
@Deepset_Fully_Normalised_Parameter_Mini
mas A

Inner Join
@Deepset_Fully_Normalised_Parameter_Maxi
mas B

        On (B.[Dataset] = A.[Dataset])

Group By A.[Dataset]
```

--The following codeblocks loads the projection granularity global variable into variables, which correspond to the sub-range transformations

```
Declare
@Projection_Sub_Range_Decimal_Percentage
Float

Set
@Projection_Sub_Range_Decimal_Percentage
=
(@Projection_Granularity_Global_Variable_Per
centage / 100)


Declare @Projection_Sub_Range_Count Float

Set @Projection_Sub_Range_Count = (100 /
@Projection_Granularity_Global_Variable_Perc
entage)
```

--The following codeblocks load the data from the fully normalised deepsets into a table variable, which corresponds to the granularised duplicate count transformation

```
Declare
@Fully_Normalised_Deepsets_With_Granularis
ed_Duplicate_Counts_Intermediate Table
([Dataset] Nvarchar(250),
[Fully_Normalised_Parameter] Float,
[Scale_Granularised_Duplicate_Count] BigInt)
```

Insert Into
@Fully_Normalised_Deepsets_With_Granularis
ed_Duplicate_Counts_Intermediate ([Dataset],
[Fully_Normalised_Parameter],
[Scale_Granularised_Duplicate_Count])

Select

A.[Dataset] As [Dataset],

A.[Fully_Normalised_Parameter] As
[Fully_Normalised_Parameter],

Count(*) As
[Scale_Granularised_Duplicate_Count]

From @Fully_Normalised_Deepsets A

Inner Join @Fully_Normalised_Deepsets B

On (B.[Dataset] = A.[Dataset] And
B.[Fully_Normalised_Parameter] >=
(A.[Fully_Normalised_Parameter] -
@Parameter_Granularity_Global_Variable_Perc
entage) And B.[Fully_Normalised_Parameter]
<= (A.[Fully_Normalised_Parameter] +
@Parameter_Granularity_Global_Variable_Perc
entage))

Inner Join @Dataset_Parameter_Counts C

On (C.[Dataset] = A.[Dataset])

Group By A.[Order], A.[Dataset],
A.[Fully_Normalised_Parameter]

--The scale-granularised duplicate count column
calculates parameter duplicate counts within a
previously set parameter granularity percentage
range either side of the parameter.

Declare
@Fully_Normalised_Deepsets_With_Granularis
ed_Duplicate_Counts_Final Table ([Dataset]
Nvarchar(250), [Fully_Normalised_Parameter]
Float, [Scale_Granularised_Duplicate_Count]
BigInt)

Insert Into
@Fully_Normalised_Deepsets_With_Granularis
ed_Duplicate_Counts_Final ([Dataset],
[Fully_Normalised_Parameter],
[Scale_Granularised_Duplicate_Count])

Select Distinct

A.[Dataset] As [Dataset],

A.[Fully_Normalised_Parameter] As
[Fully_Normalised_Parameter],

A.[Scale_Granularised_Duplicate_Count
] As [Scale_Granularised_Duplicate_Count]

```
From
@Fully_Normalised_Deepsets_With_Granularis
ed_Duplicate_Counts_Intermediate A
```

--The following codeblock determines the number of sub-ranges generated for the distribution mesh search projection.

```
Declare @Cache_Creation_Size BigInt
```

```
Set @Cache_Creation_Size =
@Projection_Sub_Range_Count
```

--The following codeblocks produce dynamically structured code in order to generate a cache row scaffold for the distribution mesh search projections.

```
Declare @Dynamic_SQL_2 Nvarchar(Max)
```

```
Set @Dynamic_SQL_2 = N'(Select
dbo.Element_Index_Generator_Code(@Parame
ter_1))'
```

```
Declare
@Dynamic_SQL_Parameter_Definition_2
Nvarchar(Max)

Set @Dynamic_SQL_Parameter_Definition_2 =
N'@Parameter_1 BigInt'


Declare
@Dynamic_SQL_Intermediate_Table_Variable_
2 Table ([Intermediate_SQL] Nvarchar(Max))

Insert Into
@Dynamic_SQL_Intermediate_Table_Variable_
2 ([Intermediate_SQL])

EXECUTE sp_executesql @Dynamic_SQL_2,
@Dynamic_SQL_Parameter_Definition_2,
@Parameter_1 = @Cache_Creation_Size


Declare @Dynamic_SQL_Intermediate_Variable
Nvarchar(Max)

Set @Dynamic_SQL_Intermediate_Variable =
(Select Replace([Intermediate_SQL],
'@Index_Count', @Cache_Creation_Size) From
@Dynamic_SQL_Intermediate_Table_Variable_
2)
```

```
Declare @Obsidian_Element_Index Table
([Element_Index] BigInt)
```

```
Insert Into @Obsidian_Element_Index
([Element_Index]) --You could just use an
existing table of integers here, which would
greatly speed up the query for big data
applications where for example billions,
trillions, or quadrillions of integers are needed
on a daily basis.
```

```
Execute
(@Dynamic_SQL_Intermediate_Variable)
```

--The following codeblock loads the projection granularity global variable into a table variable, which corresponds to the projection datapoint scaffold

```
Declare @Obsidian_Distribution_Mesh_Search
Table ([Dataset] Nvarchar(250), [Datapoint]
Float)
```

```
Insert Into
@Obsidian_Distribution_Mesh_Search
([Dataset], [Datapoint])
```

```
Select
```

```
        B.[Dataset] As [Dataset],

    (A.[Element_Index] *
@Projection_Granularity_Global_Variable_Perc
entage) As [Datapoint]

From @Obsidian_Element_Index A

Cross Join @Dataset_Parameter_Counts B
```

--The following codeblocks load the projection datapoint scaffolds into multiple table variables, which correspond to the baseline distribution mesh search transformations

--(100% is the core value you must calculate from. In addition to this, you need to assign a mean or closest lesser sample, and a mean or closest greater sample to each projection datapoint, in order to deal with duplicate values properly. As you can see, the synthesis of the duplicate data requires the application of a sample parameter duplication granularity range. On top of this, you must apply a total of 11 complex concave and convex sigmoid methods in order to generate smooth s-curve confidence percentages for projection datapoints which are not contained within the sample dataset. You must naturalise these sigmoid confidence percentages. Make sure to also include depression softening within the raw confidence method, which relies on the relationship between depression range and dataset range, given a polarised boundary minima and maxima confidence. Additionally, you need to split polarise these convex and concave spot confidence methods, so that they form curves across density depression ranges where there are no sample parameters present.)

Declare @Mean_Or_Closest_Lesser_Sample Table ([Dataset] Nvarchar(250), [Datapoint] Float, [Distribution_Mesh_Search] Float)

Insert Into @Mean_Or_Closest_Lesser_Sample ([Dataset], [Datapoint], [Distribution_Mesh_Search])

Select

      A.[Dataset] As [Dataset],

      A.[Datapoint] As [Datapoint],

      Max(B.[Fully_Normalised_Parameter]) As [Distribution_Mesh_Search]

From @Obsidian_Distribution_Mesh_Search A

```
Inner Join
@Fully_Normalised_Deepsets_With_Granularis
ed_Duplicate_Counts_Final B

        On (B.[Dataset] = A.[Dataset] And
B.[Fully_Normalised_Parameter] <=
A.[Datapoint])

Group By A.[Dataset], A.[Datapoint]



Declare @Mean_Or_Closest_Greater_Sample
Table ([Dataset] Nvarchar(250), [Datapoint]
Float, [Distribution_Mesh_Search] Float)

Insert Into
@Mean_Or_Closest_Greater_Sample
([Dataset], [Datapoint],
[Distribution_Mesh_Search])

Select

        A.[Dataset] As [Dataset],

        A.[Datapoint] As [Datapoint],

        Min(B.[Fully_Normalised_Parameter])
As [Distribution_Mesh_Search]

From @Obsidian_Distribution_Mesh_Search A
```

```
Inner Join
@Fully_Normalised_Deepsets_With_Granularis
ed_Duplicate_Counts_Final B

        On (B.[Dataset] = A.[Dataset] And
B.[Fully_Normalised_Parameter] >=
A.[Datapoint]) --It seems there is a showstopper
```

bug here in my current version of the SQL Server engine (2019). There is a valid join missing for the >= operator for A.[Datapoint] = 100, and also the >= join feature is missing the lower end of the join range for A.[Datapoint] = 50 (which should join to another 50 in the B alias table but doesn't)!

```
Group By A.[Dataset], A.[Datapoint]



Declare
@Outer_Sigmoid_Alpha_Density_Confidence_P
ercentage Table ([Dataset] Nvarchar(250),
[Datapoint] Float, [Distribution_Mesh_Search]
Float)

Insert Into
@Outer_Sigmoid_Alpha_Density_Confidence_P
ercentage ([Dataset], [Datapoint],
[Distribution_Mesh_Search])

Select

        A.[Dataset] As [Dataset],
```

A.[Datapoint] As [Datapoint],

(Sqrt(Power((D.[Scale_Granularised_Du
plicate_Count] * (Case When
C.[Distribution_Mesh_Search] =
B.[Distribution_Mesh_Search] Then 1 Else
((A.[Datapoint] - B.[Distribution_Mesh_Search])
/ (C.[Distribution_Mesh_Search] -
B.[Distribution_Mesh_Search])) End)), 2)) /
E.[Parameter_Count]) As
[Distribution_Mesh_Search]

From @Obsidian_Distribution_Mesh_Search A

Inner Join @Mean_Or_Closest_Lesser_Sample
B

On (B.[Dataset] = A.[Dataset] And
B.[Datapoint] = A.[Datapoint])

Inner Join @Mean_Or_Closest_Greater_Sample
C

On (C.[Dataset] = A.[Dataset] And
C.[Datapoint] = A.[Datapoint])

Inner Join
@Fully_Normalised_Deepsets_With_Granularis
ed_Duplicate_Counts_Final D

On (D.[Dataset] = A.[Dataset] And
D.[Fully_Normalised_Parameter] =
B.[Distribution_Mesh_Search])

Inner Join @Dataset_Parameter_Counts E

On (E.[Dataset] = A.[Dataset])

Declare @Inner_Sigmoid_Alpha_Density_Confidence_Percentage Table ([Dataset] Nvarchar(250), [Datapoint] Float, [Distribution_Mesh_Search] Float)

Insert Into @Inner_Sigmoid_Alpha_Density_Confidence_Percentage ([Dataset], [Datapoint], [Distribution_Mesh_Search])

Select

      A.[Dataset] As [Dataset],

      A.[Datapoint] As [Datapoint],

      (Sqrt(Power((D.[Scale_Granularised_Duplicate_Count] * (Case When C.[Distribution_Mesh_Search] = B.[Distribution_Mesh_Search] Then 1 Else ((A.[Datapoint] - B.[Distribution_Mesh_Search]) / (C.[Distribution_Mesh_Search] - B.[Distribution_Mesh_Search])) End)), 2)) / E.[Parameter_Count]) As [Distribution_Mesh_Search]

From @Obsidian_Distribution_Mesh_Search A

Inner Join @Mean_Or_Closest_Lesser_Sample B

On (B.[Dataset] = A.[Dataset] And B.[Datapoint] = A.[Datapoint])

Inner Join @Mean_Or_Closest_Greater_Sample C

On (C.[Dataset] = A.[Dataset] And C.[Datapoint] = A.[Datapoint])

Inner Join @Fully_Normalised_Deepsets_With_Granularised_Duplicate_Counts_Final D

On (D.[Dataset] = A.[Dataset] And D.[Fully_Normalised_Parameter] = C.[Distribution_Mesh_Search])

Inner Join @Dataset_Parameter_Counts E

On (E.[Dataset] = A.[Dataset])

Declare @Outer_Sigmoid_Beta_Density_Confidence_Percentage Table ([Dataset] Nvarchar(250), [Datapoint] Float, [Distribution_Mesh_Search] Float)

Insert Into
@Outer_Sigmoid_Beta_Density_Confidence_Pe
rcentage ([Dataset], [Datapoint],
[Distribution_Mesh_Search])

Select

A.[Dataset] As [Dataset],

A.[Datapoint] As [Datapoint],

(Sqrt(Power((D.[Scale_Granularised_Du
plicate_Count] * (Case When
C.[Distribution_Mesh_Search] =
B.[Distribution_Mesh_Search] Then 1 Else
((C.[Distribution_Mesh_Search] - A.[Datapoint])
/ (C.[Distribution_Mesh_Search] -
B.[Distribution_Mesh_Search])) End)), 2)) /
E.[Parameter_Count]) As
[Distribution_Mesh_Search]

From @Obsidian_Distribution_Mesh_Search A

Inner Join @Mean_Or_Closest_Lesser_Sample
B

On (B.[Dataset] = A.[Dataset] And
B.[Datapoint] = A.[Datapoint])

Inner Join @Mean_Or_Closest_Greater_Sample
C

On (C.[Dataset] = A.[Dataset] And
C.[Datapoint] = A.[Datapoint])

Inner Join
@Fully_Normalised_Deepsets_With_Granularis
ed_Duplicate_Counts_Final D

On (D.[Dataset] = A.[Dataset] And
D.[Fully_Normalised_Parameter] =
B.[Distribution_Mesh_Search])

Inner Join @Dataset_Parameter_Counts E

On (E.[Dataset] = A.[Dataset])

Declare
@Inner_Sigmoid_Beta_Density_Confidence_Per
centage Table ([Dataset] Nvarchar(250),
[Datapoint] Float, [Distribution_Mesh_Search]
Float)

Insert Into
@Inner_Sigmoid_Beta_Density_Confidence_Per
centage ([Dataset], [Datapoint],
[Distribution_Mesh_Search])

Select

A.[Dataset] As [Dataset],

A.[Datapoint] As [Datapoint],

(Sqrt(Power((D.[Scale_Granularised_Du
plicate_Count] * (Case When
C.[Distribution_Mesh_Search] =
B.[Distribution_Mesh_Search] Then 1 Else
((C.[Distribution_Mesh_Search] - A.[Datapoint])
/ (C.[Distribution_Mesh_Search] -
B.[Distribution_Mesh_Search])) End)), 2)) /
E.[Parameter_Count]) As
[Distribution_Mesh_Search]

From @Obsidian_Distribution_Mesh_Search A

Inner Join @Mean_Or_Closest_Lesser_Sample
B

On (B.[Dataset] = A.[Dataset] And
B.[Datapoint] = A.[Datapoint])

Inner Join @Mean_Or_Closest_Greater_Sample
C

On (C.[Dataset] = A.[Dataset] And
C.[Datapoint] = A.[Datapoint])

Inner Join
@Fully_Normalised_Deepsets_With_Granularis
ed_Duplicate_Counts_Final D

On (D.[Dataset] = A.[Dataset] And
D.[Fully_Normalised_Parameter] =
C.[Distribution_Mesh_Search])

Inner Join @Dataset_Parameter_Counts E

On (E.[Dataset] = A.[Dataset])

Declare
@Boundary_Projection_Convex_Spot_Confiden
ce_Percentage_Coalesce Table ([Dataset]
Nvarchar(250), [Datapoint] Float,
[Distribution_Mesh_Search_Coalesce] Float)

Insert Into
@Boundary_Projection_Convex_Spot_Confiden
ce_Percentage_Coalesce ([Dataset],
[Datapoint],
[Distribution_Mesh_Search_Coalesce])

Select

A.[Dataset] As [Dataset],

A.[Datapoint] As [Datapoint],

B.[Distribution_Mesh_Search] As
[Distribution_Mesh_Search_Coalesce]

From @Obsidian_Distribution_Mesh_Search A

Inner Join
@Outer_Sigmoid_Alpha_Density_Confidence_P
ercentage B

On (B.[Dataset] = A.[Dataset] And
B.[Datapoint] = A.[Datapoint])

Union All

Select

        A.[Dataset] As [Dataset],

        A.[Datapoint] As [Datapoint],

        B.[Distribution_Mesh_Search] As [Distribution_Mesh_Search_Coalesce]

From @Obsidian_Distribution_Mesh_Search A

Inner Join @Inner_Sigmoid_Alpha_Density_Confidence_Percentage B

        On (B.[Dataset] = A.[Dataset] And B.[Datapoint] = A.[Datapoint])

Union All

Select

        A.[Dataset] As [Dataset],

        A.[Datapoint] As [Datapoint],

        B.[Distribution_Mesh_Search] As [Distribution_Mesh_Search_Coalesce]

From @Obsidian_Distribution_Mesh_Search A

Inner Join @Outer_Sigmoid_Beta_Density_Confidence_Percentage B

```
        On (B.[Dataset] = A.[Dataset] And
B.[Datapoint] = A.[Datapoint])

Union All

Select

        A.[Dataset] As [Dataset],

        A.[Datapoint] As [Datapoint],

        B.[Distribution_Mesh_Search] As
[Distribution_Mesh_Search_Coalesce]

From @Obsidian_Distribution_Mesh_Search A

Inner Join
@Inner_Sigmoid_Beta_Density_Confidence_Per
centage B

        On (B.[Dataset] = A.[Dataset] And
B.[Datapoint] = A.[Datapoint])


Declare
@Boundary_Projection_Convex_Spot_Confiden
ce_Percentage_Minimum Table ([Dataset]
Nvarchar(250), [Datapoint] Float,
[Distribution_Mesh_Search_Minimum] Float)

Insert Into
@Boundary_Projection_Convex_Spot_Confiden
ce_Percentage_Minimum ([Dataset],
```

```
[Datapoint],
[Distribution_Mesh_Search_Minimum])
```

Select

```
        [Dataset] As [Dataset],

        [Datapoint] As [Datapoint],

        Min([Distribution_Mesh_Search_Coales
ce]) As [Distribution_Mesh_Search_Minimum]
```

From
@Boundary_Projection_Convex_Spot_Confiden
ce_Percentage_Coalesce

Group By [Dataset], [Datapoint]

Declare
@Boundary_Projection_Convex_Spot_Confiden
ce_Percentage_Maximum Table ([Dataset]
Nvarchar(250), [Datapoint] Float,
[Distribution_Mesh_Search_Maximum] Float)

Insert Into
@Boundary_Projection_Convex_Spot_Confiden
ce_Percentage_Maximum ([Dataset],
[Datapoint],
[Distribution_Mesh_Search_Maximum])

Select

```
        [Dataset] As [Dataset],

        [Datapoint] As [Datapoint],

        Max([Distribution_Mesh_Search_Coales
ce]) As [Distribution_Mesh_Search_Minimum]

From
@Boundary_Projection_Convex_Spot_Confiden
ce_Percentage_Coalesce

Group By [Dataset], [Datapoint]



Declare
@Lower_Boundary_Projection_Convex_Spot_C
onfidence_Percentage_Final Table ([Dataset]
Nvarchar(250), [Datapoint] Float,
[Distribution_Mesh_Search] Float)

Insert Into
@Lower_Boundary_Projection_Convex_Spot_C
onfidence_Percentage_Final ([Dataset],
[Datapoint], [Distribution_Mesh_Search])

Select

        A.[Dataset] As [Dataset],

        A.[Datapoint] As [Datapoint],

        (Case When
C.[Distribution_Mesh_Search] =
```

B.[Distribution_Mesh_Search] Then
A.[Distribution_Mesh_Search_Minimum] Else
(D.[Distribution_Mesh_Search] +
F.[Distribution_Mesh_Search]) End) As
[Distribution_Mesh_Search]

From
@Boundary_Projection_Convex_Spot_Confiden
ce_Percentage_Minimum A

Inner Join @Mean_Or_Closest_Lesser_Sample
B

      On (B.[Dataset] = A.[Dataset] And
B.[Datapoint] = A.[Datapoint])

Inner Join @Mean_Or_Closest_Greater_Sample
C

      On (C.[Dataset] = A.[Dataset] And
C.[Datapoint] = A.[Datapoint])

Inner Join
@Outer_Sigmoid_Alpha_Density_Confidence_P
ercentage D

      On (D.[Dataset] = A.[Dataset] And
D.[Datapoint] = A.[Datapoint])

Inner Join
@Inner_Sigmoid_Alpha_Density_Confidence_P
ercentage E

```
        On (E.[Dataset] = A.[Dataset] And
E.[Datapoint] = A.[Datapoint])

Inner Join
@Outer_Sigmoid_Beta_Density_Confidence_Pe
rcentage F

        On (F.[Dataset] = A.[Dataset] And
F.[Datapoint] = A.[Datapoint])

Inner Join
@Inner_Sigmoid_Beta_Density_Confidence_Per
centage G

        On (G.[Dataset] = A.[Dataset] And
G.[Datapoint] = A.[Datapoint])



Declare
@Upper_Boundary_Projection_Convex_Spot_C
onfidence_Percentage_Final Table ([Dataset]
Nvarchar(250), [Datapoint] Float,
[Distribution_Mesh_Search] Float)

Insert Into
@Upper_Boundary_Projection_Convex_Spot_C
onfidence_Percentage_Final ([Dataset],
[Datapoint], [Distribution_Mesh_Search])

Select

        A.[Dataset] As [Dataset],
```

A.[Datapoint] As [Datapoint],

(Case When
C.[Distribution_Mesh_Search] =
B.[Distribution_Mesh_Search] Then
A.[Distribution_Mesh_Search_Maximum] Else
(E.[Distribution_Mesh_Search] +
G.[Distribution_Mesh_Search]) End) As
[Distribution_Mesh_Search]

From
@Boundary_Projection_Convex_Spot_Confiden
ce_Percentage_Maximum A

Inner Join @Mean_Or_Closest_Lesser_Sample
B

     On (B.[Dataset] = A.[Dataset] And
B.[Datapoint] = A.[Datapoint])

Inner Join @Mean_Or_Closest_Greater_Sample
C

     On (C.[Dataset] = A.[Dataset] And
C.[Datapoint] = A.[Datapoint])

Inner Join
@Outer_Sigmoid_Alpha_Density_Confidence_P
ercentage D

     On (D.[Dataset] = A.[Dataset] And
D.[Datapoint] = A.[Datapoint])

Inner Join
@Inner_Sigmoid_Alpha_Density_Confidence_P
ercentage E

    On (E.[Dataset] = A.[Dataset] And
E.[Datapoint] = A.[Datapoint])

Inner Join
@Outer_Sigmoid_Beta_Density_Confidence_Pe
rcentage F

    On (F.[Dataset] = A.[Dataset] And
F.[Datapoint] = A.[Datapoint])

Inner Join
@Inner_Sigmoid_Beta_Density_Confidence_Per
centage G

    On (G.[Dataset] = A.[Dataset] And
G.[Datapoint] = A.[Datapoint])

Declare
@Raw_Depression_Polarised_Boundary_Minim
a_Spot_Confidence_Percentage Table
([Dataset] Nvarchar(250), [Datapoint] Float,
[Distribution_Mesh_Search] Float)

Insert Into
@Raw_Depression_Polarised_Boundary_Minim
a_Spot_Confidence_Percentage ([Dataset],
[Datapoint], [Distribution_Mesh_Search])

Select

    A.[Dataset] As [Dataset],

    A.[Datapoint] As [Datapoint],

    ((D.[Distribution_Mesh_Search] * ((Case When C.[Distribution_Mesh_Search] = B.[Distribution_Mesh_Search] Then 0.5 Else (C.[Distribution_Mesh_Search] - A.[Datapoint]) End) / (Case When C.[Distribution_Mesh_Search] = B.[Distribution_Mesh_Search] Then 1 Else (C.[Distribution_Mesh_Search] - B.[Distribution_Mesh_Search]) End))) + (E.[Distribution_Mesh_Search] * ((Case When C.[Distribution_Mesh_Search] = B.[Distribution_Mesh_Search] Then 0.5 Else (A.[Datapoint] - B.[Distribution_Mesh_Search]) End) / (Case When C.[Distribution_Mesh_Search] = B.[Distribution_Mesh_Search] Then 1 Else (C.[Distribution_Mesh_Search] - B.[Distribution_Mesh_Search]) End)))) As [Distribution_Mesh_Search]

From @Obsidian_Distribution_Mesh_Search A

Inner Join @Mean_Or_Closest_Lesser_Sample B

```
        On (B.[Dataset] = A.[Dataset] And
B.[Datapoint] = A.[Datapoint])

Inner Join @Mean_Or_Closest_Greater_Sample
C

        On (C.[Dataset] = A.[Dataset] And
C.[Datapoint] = A.[Datapoint])

Inner Join
@Lower_Boundary_Projection_Convex_Spot_C
onfidence_Percentage_Final  D

        On (D.[Dataset] = A.[Dataset] And
D.[Datapoint] = A.[Datapoint])

Inner Join
@Upper_Boundary_Projection_Convex_Spot_C
onfidence_Percentage_Final E

        On (E.[Dataset] = A.[Dataset] And
E.[Datapoint] = A.[Datapoint])


Declare
@Projection_Convex_Spot_Confidence_Percent
age Table ([Dataset] Nvarchar(250), [Datapoint]
Float, [Distribution_Mesh_Search] Float)

Insert Into
@Projection_Convex_Spot_Confidence_Percent
```

age ([Dataset], [Datapoint],
[Distribution_Mesh_Search])

Select

      A.[Dataset] As [Dataset],

      A.[Datapoint] As [Datapoint],

      (Case When
C.[Distribution_Mesh_Search] =
B.[Distribution_Mesh_Search] Then
A.[Distribution_Mesh_Search_Maximum] Else
(((D.[Distribution_Mesh_Search] * (1 -
((A.[Datapoint] - B.[Distribution_Mesh_Search])
/ (C.[Distribution_Mesh_Search] -
B.[Distribution_Mesh_Search]))))) *
((C.[Distribution_Mesh_Search] - A.[Datapoint])
/ (C.[Distribution_Mesh_Search] -
B.[Distribution_Mesh_Search])))) +
((E.[Distribution_Mesh_Search] * (1 -
((C.[Distribution_Mesh_Search] - A.[Datapoint])
/ (C.[Distribution_Mesh_Search] -
B.[Distribution_Mesh_Search])))) *
((A.[Datapoint] - B.[Distribution_Mesh_Search])
/ (C.[Distribution_Mesh_Search] -
B.[Distribution_Mesh_Search]))) +
((F.[Distribution_Mesh_Search] * (1 -
((A.[Datapoint] - B.[Distribution_Mesh_Search])
/ (C.[Distribution_Mesh_Search] -
B.[Distribution_Mesh_Search])))) *

((C.[Distribution_Mesh_Search] - A.[Datapoint])
/ (C.[Distribution_Mesh_Search] -
B.[Distribution_Mesh_Search]))) +
((G.[Distribution_Mesh_Search] * (1 -
((C.[Distribution_Mesh_Search] - A.[Datapoint])
/ (C.[Distribution_Mesh_Search] -
B.[Distribution_Mesh_Search])))) *
((A.[Datapoint] - B.[Distribution_Mesh_Search])
/ (C.[Distribution_Mesh_Search] -
B.[Distribution_Mesh_Search])))) End) As
[Distribution_Mesh_Search]

From
@Boundary_Projection_Convex_Spot_Confiden
ce_Percentage_Maximum A

Inner Join @Mean_Or_Closest_Lesser_Sample
B

On (B.[Dataset] = A.[Dataset] And
B.[Datapoint] = A.[Datapoint])

Inner Join @Mean_Or_Closest_Greater_Sample
C

On (C.[Dataset] = A.[Dataset] And
C.[Datapoint] = A.[Datapoint])

Inner Join
@Outer_Sigmoid_Alpha_Density_Confidence_P
ercentage D

```
        On (D.[Dataset] = A.[Dataset] And
D.[Datapoint] = A.[Datapoint])

Inner Join
@Inner_Sigmoid_Alpha_Density_Confidence_P
ercentage E

        On (E.[Dataset] = A.[Dataset] And
E.[Datapoint] = A.[Datapoint])

Inner Join
@Outer_Sigmoid_Beta_Density_Confidence_Pe
rcentage F

        On (F.[Dataset] = A.[Dataset] And
F.[Datapoint] = A.[Datapoint])

Inner Join
@Inner_Sigmoid_Beta_Density_Confidence_Per
centage G

        On (G.[Dataset] = A.[Dataset] And
G.[Datapoint] = A.[Datapoint])


Declare
@Projection_Concave_Spot_Confidence_Perce
ntage Table ([Dataset] Nvarchar(250),
[Datapoint] Float, [Distribution_Mesh_Search]
Float)
```

Insert Into
@Projection_Concave_Spot_Confidence_Perce
ntage ([Dataset], [Datapoint],
[Distribution_Mesh_Search])

Select

A.[Dataset] As [Dataset],

A.[Datapoint] As [Datapoint],

(Case When
C.[Distribution_Mesh_Search] =
B.[Distribution_Mesh_Search] Then 0 Else
(((D.[Distribution_Mesh_Search] *
((A.[Datapoint] - B.[Distribution_Mesh_Search])
/ (C.[Distribution_Mesh_Search] -
B.[Distribution_Mesh_Search]))) *
((C.[Distribution_Mesh_Search] - A.[Datapoint])
/ (C.[Distribution_Mesh_Search] -
B.[Distribution_Mesh_Search]))) +
((E.[Distribution_Mesh_Search] *
((C.[Distribution_Mesh_Search] - A.[Datapoint])
/ (C.[Distribution_Mesh_Search] -
B.[Distribution_Mesh_Search]))) *
((A.[Datapoint] - B.[Distribution_Mesh_Search])
/ (C.[Distribution_Mesh_Search] -
B.[Distribution_Mesh_Search]))) +
((F.[Distribution_Mesh_Search] *
((A.[Datapoint] - B.[Distribution_Mesh_Search])
/ (C.[Distribution_Mesh_Search] -

B.[Distribution_Mesh_Search]))) *
((C.[Distribution_Mesh_Search] - A.[Datapoint])
/ (C.[Distribution_Mesh_Search] -
B.[Distribution_Mesh_Search]))) +
((G.[Distribution_Mesh_Search] *
((C.[Distribution_Mesh_Search] - A.[Datapoint])
/ (C.[Distribution_Mesh_Search] -
B.[Distribution_Mesh_Search]))) *
((A.[Datapoint] - B.[Distribution_Mesh_Search])
/ (C.[Distribution_Mesh_Search] -
B.[Distribution_Mesh_Search]))))) End) As
[Distribution_Mesh_Search]

From @Obsidian_Distribution_Mesh_Search A

Inner Join @Mean_Or_Closest_Lesser_Sample
B

    On (B.[Dataset] = A.[Dataset] And
B.[Datapoint] = A.[Datapoint])

Inner Join @Mean_Or_Closest_Greater_Sample
C

    On (C.[Dataset] = A.[Dataset] And
C.[Datapoint] = A.[Datapoint])

Inner Join
@Outer_Sigmoid_Alpha_Density_Confidence_P
ercentage D

    On (D.[Dataset] = A.[Dataset] And
D.[Datapoint] = A.[Datapoint])

```
Inner Join
@Inner_Sigmoid_Alpha_Density_Confidence_P
ercentage E

        On (E.[Dataset] = A.[Dataset] And
E.[Datapoint] = A.[Datapoint])

Inner Join
@Outer_Sigmoid_Beta_Density_Confidence_Pe
rcentage F

        On (F.[Dataset] = A.[Dataset] And
F.[Datapoint] = A.[Datapoint])

Inner Join
@Inner_Sigmoid_Beta_Density_Confidence_Per
centage G

        On (G.[Dataset] = A.[Dataset] And
G.[Datapoint] = A.[Datapoint])


Declare
@Split_Polarity_Of_Density_Depression Table
([Dataset] Nvarchar(250), [Datapoint] Float,
[Distribution_Mesh_Search] Float)

Insert Into
@Split_Polarity_Of_Density_Depression
([Dataset], [Datapoint],
[Distribution_Mesh_Search])
```

```
Select

        A.[Dataset] As [Dataset],

        A.[Datapoint] As [Datapoint],

        (((Case When
C.[Distribution_Mesh_Search] =
B.[Distribution_Mesh_Search] Then 1 Else (Case
When A.[Datapoint] <=
(B.[Distribution_Mesh_Search] +
((C.[Distribution_Mesh_Search] -
B.[Distribution_Mesh_Search]) / 2)) Then (1 -
Sqrt(Power(((A.[Datapoint] -
B.[Distribution_Mesh_Search]) /
(C.[Distribution_Mesh_Search] -
B.[Distribution_Mesh_Search])), 2))) Else
Sqrt(Power(((A.[Datapoint] -
B.[Distribution_Mesh_Search]) /
(C.[Distribution_Mesh_Search] -
B.[Distribution_Mesh_Search])), 2)) End) End) -
0.5) * 2) As [Distribution_Mesh_Search]

From @Obsidian_Distribution_Mesh_Search A

Inner Join @Mean_Or_Closest_Lesser_Sample
B

        On (B.[Dataset] = A.[Dataset] And
B.[Datapoint] = A.[Datapoint])

Inner Join @Mean_Or_Closest_Greater_Sample
C
```

```
        On (C.[Dataset] = A.[Dataset] And
C.[Datapoint] = A.[Datapoint])


Declare
@Projection_Spot_Confidence_Percentage
Table ([Dataset] Nvarchar(250), [Datapoint]
Float, [Distribution_Mesh_Search] Float)

Insert Into
@Projection_Spot_Confidence_Percentage
([Dataset], [Datapoint],
[Distribution_Mesh_Search])

Select

        A.[Dataset] As [Dataset],

        A.[Datapoint] As [Datapoint],

        (((((E.[Distribution_Mesh_Search] * ((1 -
G.[Distribution_Mesh_Search]) * (Case When
B.[Distribution_Mesh_Search] =
C.[Distribution_Mesh_Search] Then 1 Else (1 -
((C.[Distribution_Mesh_Search] -
B.[Distribution_Mesh_Search]) /
H.[Parameter_Range])) End))) +
((E.[Distribution_Mesh_Search] + ((Case When
((C.[Distribution_Mesh_Search] -
B.[Distribution_Mesh_Search]) /
H.[Parameter_Range]) = 1 Then
F.[Distribution_Mesh_Search] Else
```

(F.[Distribution_Mesh_Search]/(Case When
B.[Distribution_Mesh_Search] =
C.[Distribution_Mesh_Search] Then 1 Else (1 -
((C.[Distribution_Mesh_Search] -
B.[Distribution_Mesh_Search]) /
H.[Parameter_Range])) End)) End) *
G.[Distribution_Mesh_Search])) *
G.[Distribution_Mesh_Search])) * (1 - ((1 -
G.[Distribution_Mesh_Search]) * (Case When
B.[Distribution_Mesh_Search] =
C.[Distribution_Mesh_Search] Then 1 Else
((C.[Distribution_Mesh_Search] -
B.[Distribution_Mesh_Search]) /
H.[Parameter_Range]) End)))) +
((D.[Distribution_Mesh_Search] -
(((E.[Distribution_Mesh_Search] * ((1 -
G.[Distribution_Mesh_Search]) * (Case When
B.[Distribution_Mesh_Search] =
C.[Distribution_Mesh_Search] Then 1 Else (1 -
((C.[Distribution_Mesh_Search] -
B.[Distribution_Mesh_Search]) /
H.[Parameter_Range])) End))) +
((E.[Distribution_Mesh_Search] + ((Case When
((C.[Distribution_Mesh_Search] -
B.[Distribution_Mesh_Search]) /
H.[Parameter_Range]) = 1 Then
F.[Distribution_Mesh_Search] Else
(F.[Distribution_Mesh_Search] / (Case When
B.[Distribution_Mesh_Search] =

C.[Distribution_Mesh_Search] Then 1 Else (1 -
((C.[Distribution_Mesh_Search] -
B.[Distribution_Mesh_Search]) /
H.[Parameter_Range])) End)) End) *
G.[Distribution_Mesh_Search])) *
G.[Distribution_Mesh_Search])) * (1 - ((1 -
G.[Distribution_Mesh_Search]) * (Case When
B.[Distribution_Mesh_Search] =
C.[Distribution_Mesh_Search] Then 1 Else
((C.[Distribution_Mesh_Search] -
B.[Distribution_Mesh_Search]) /
H.[Parameter_Range]) End)))) * (1 -
((C.[Distribution_Mesh_Search] -
B.[Distribution_Mesh_Search]) /
H.[Parameter_Range])))) * 100) As
[Distribution_Mesh_Search]

From @Obsidian_Distribution_Mesh_Search A

Inner Join @Mean_Or_Closest_Lesser_Sample
B

    On (B.[Dataset] = A.[Dataset] And
B.[Datapoint] = A.[Datapoint])

Inner Join @Mean_Or_Closest_Greater_Sample
C

    On (C.[Dataset] = A.[Dataset] And
C.[Datapoint] = A.[Datapoint])

Inner Join
@Raw_Depression_Polarised_Boundary_Minim
a_Spot_Confidence_Percentage D

On (D.[Dataset] = A.[Dataset] And
D.[Datapoint] = A.[Datapoint])

Inner Join
@Projection_Convex_Spot_Confidence_Percent
age E

On (E.[Dataset] = A.[Dataset] And
E.[Datapoint] = A.[Datapoint])

Inner Join
@Projection_Concave_Spot_Confidence_Perce
ntage F

On (F.[Dataset] = A.[Dataset] And
F.[Datapoint] = A.[Datapoint])

Inner Join
@Split_Polarity_Of_Density_Depression G

On (G.[Dataset] = A.[Dataset] And
G.[Datapoint] = A.[Datapoint])

Inner Join
@Deepset_Fully_Normalised_Parameter_Range
s H

On (H.[Dataset] = A.[Dataset])

--The following codeblocks load the baseline distribution mesh search into multiple table variables, which correspond to the compositional model-phase transition probability inference transformations

```
Declare
@Limit_Normalised_Projection_Datapoint_Reg
ulariser Table ([Dataset] Nvarchar(250),
[Datapoint] Float,
[Minimum_Regularised_Datapoint] Float,
[Middle_Regularised_Datapoint] Float,
[Maximum_Regularised_Datapoint] Float)

Insert Into
@Limit_Normalised_Projection_Datapoint_Reg
ulariser ([Dataset], [Datapoint],
[Minimum_Regularised_Datapoint],
[Middle_Regularised_Datapoint],
[Maximum_Regularised_Datapoint])

Select

        A.[Dataset] As [Dataset],

        A.[Datapoint] As [Datapoint],

        Min(Case When
(C.[Distribution_Mesh_Search] -
B.[Distribution_Mesh_Search]) >
@Exploding_Probability_Gradient_Dataset_Ran
```

ge_Limit_Percentage Then (Case When
A.[Datapoint] < ((C.[Distribution_Mesh_Search]
+ B.[Distribution_Mesh_Search]) / 2) Then (Case
When A.[Distribution_Mesh_Search] >
D.[Distribution_Mesh_Search] Then
B.[Distribution_Mesh_Search] Else
/*Regularised Trough -->*/ -1 End) Else Null
End) Else A.[Datapoint] End) As
[Minimum_Regularised_Datapoint],

Avg(Case When
(C.[Distribution_Mesh_Search] -
B.[Distribution_Mesh_Search]) >
@Exploding_Probability_Gradient_Dataset_Ran
ge_Limit_Percentage Then (Case When
A.[Datapoint] = ((C.[Distribution_Mesh_Search]
+ B.[Distribution_Mesh_Search]) / 2) Then
/*Regularised Trough -->*/ -1 Else Null End) Else
A.[Datapoint] End) As
[Middle_Regularised_Datapoint],

Max(Case When
(C.[Distribution_Mesh_Search] -
B.[Distribution_Mesh_Search]) >
@Exploding_Probability_Gradient_Dataset_Ran
ge_Limit_Percentage Then (Case When
A.[Datapoint] > ((C.[Distribution_Mesh_Search]
+ B.[Distribution_Mesh_Search]) / 2) Then (Case
When A.[Distribution_Mesh_Search] >
D.[Distribution_Mesh_Search] Then

C.[Distribution_Mesh_Search] Else
/*Regularised Trough -->*/ -1 End) Else Null
End) Else A.[Datapoint] End) As
[Maximum_Regularised_Datapoint]

From
@Projection_Spot_Confidence_Percentage A

Inner Join @Mean_Or_Closest_Lesser_Sample
B

    On (B.[Dataset] = A.[Dataset] And
B.[Datapoint] = A.[Datapoint])

Inner Join @Mean_Or_Closest_Greater_Sample
C

    On (C.[Dataset] = A.[Dataset] And
C.[Datapoint] = A.[Datapoint])

Inner Join
@Projection_Spot_Confidence_Percentage D

    On (D.[Dataset] = A.[Dataset] And
D.[Datapoint] >= B.[Distribution_Mesh_Search]
And D.[Datapoint] <=
C.[Distribution_Mesh_Search])

Group By A.[Dataset], A.[Datapoint]

--This table variable transformation regularises
the baseline probabilities in order to find
exploding gradient datapoints.

```
Declare
@Model_Phase_Transitioned_Projection_Spot_
Confidence_Percentage_Intermediate Table
([Dataset] Nvarchar(250), [Datapoint] Float,
[Spot_Confidence] Float)

Insert Into
@Model_Phase_Transitioned_Projection_Spot_
Confidence_Percentage_Intermediate
([Dataset], [Datapoint], [Spot_Confidence])

Select --Coalesce sub-liminal peak exploding
gradient datapoints.

        A1.[Dataset] As [Dataset],

        A1.[Datapoint] As [Datapoint],

        D1.[Distribution_Mesh_Search] As
[Spot_Confidence]

From
@Limit_Normalised_Projection_Datapoint_Reg
ulariser A1

Inner Join @Mean_Or_Closest_Lesser_Sample
B1

        On (B1.[Dataset] = A1.[Dataset] And
B1.[Datapoint] = A1.[Datapoint])
```

Inner Join @Mean_Or_Closest_Greater_Sample
C1

      On (C1.[Dataset] = A1.[Dataset] And
C1.[Datapoint] = A1.[Datapoint])

Inner Join
@Projection_Spot_Confidence_Percentage D1 -
-I believe that there is a showstopper critical
SQL Server 2019 engine bug here. There are
(And D1.[Datapoint] =
A1.[Minimum_Regularised_Datapoint]) joins
missing.

      On (D1.[Dataset] = A1.[Dataset] And
D1.[Datapoint] =
A1.[Minimum_Regularised_Datapoint] And
A1.[Datapoint] <
((B1.[Distribution_Mesh_Search] +
C1.[Distribution_Mesh_Search]) / 2) And
A1.[Minimum_Regularised_Datapoint] <> -1
And A1.[Middle_Regularised_Datapoint] Is Null
And A1.[Maximum_Regularised_Datapoint] Is
Null)

Union All

Select --Coalesce super-liminal peak exploding
gradient datapoints.

      A2.[Dataset] As [Dataset],

      A2.[Datapoint] As [Datapoint],

D2.[Distribution_Mesh_Search] As [Spot_Confidence]

From @Limit_Normalised_Projection_Datapoint_Regulariser A2

Inner Join @Mean_Or_Closest_Lesser_Sample B2

On (B2.[Dataset] = A2.[Dataset] And B2.[Datapoint] = A2.[Datapoint])

Inner Join @Mean_Or_Closest_Greater_Sample C2

On (C2.[Dataset] = A2.[Dataset] And C2.[Datapoint] = A2.[Datapoint])

Inner Join @Projection_Spot_Confidence_Percentage D2 - -I believe that there is a showstopper critical SQL Server 2019 engine bug here. There are (And D1.[Datapoint] = A2.[Maximum_Regularised_Datapoint]) joins missing... This is probably the same bug mentioned earlier in this coalesced union all selection, for sub-liminal peak exploding gradient datapoints.

On (D2.[Dataset] = A2.[Dataset] And D2.[Datapoint] = A2.[Maximum_Regularised_Datapoint] And

A2.[Datapoint] >
((B2.[Distribution_Mesh_Search] +
C2.[Distribution_Mesh_Search]) / 2) And
A2.[Maximum_Regularised_Datapoint] <> -1
And A2.[Minimum_Regularised_Datapoint] Is
Null And A2.[Middle_Regularised_Datapoint] Is
Null)

Union All

Select --Coalesce sub-liminal, mid-liminal, and
super-liminal trough imploding gradient
datapoints.

    A3.[Dataset] As [Dataset],

    A3.[Datapoint] As [Datapoint],

    Min(D3.[Distribution_Mesh_Search]) As
[Spot_Confidence]

From
@Limit_Normalised_Projection_Datapoint_Reg
ulariser A3

Inner Join @Mean_Or_Closest_Lesser_Sample
B3

    On (B3.[Dataset] = A3.[Dataset] And
B3.[Datapoint] = A3.[Datapoint])

Inner Join @Mean_Or_Closest_Greater_Sample
C3

```
        On (C3.[Dataset] = A3.[Dataset] And
C3.[Datapoint] = A3.[Datapoint])

Inner Join
@Projection_Spot_Confidence_Percentage D3

        On (D3.[Dataset] = A3.[Dataset] And
D3.[Datapoint] >=
B3.[Distribution_Mesh_Search] And
D3.[Datapoint] <=
C3.[Distribution_Mesh_Search] And
A3.[Minimum_Regularised_Datapoint] = -1 Or
D3.[Dataset] = A3.[Dataset] And D3.[Datapoint]
>= B3.[Distribution_Mesh_Search] And
D3.[Datapoint] <=
C3.[Distribution_Mesh_Search] And
A3.[Middle_Regularised_Datapoint] = -1 Or
D3.[Dataset] = A3.[Dataset] And D3.[Datapoint]
>= B3.[Distribution_Mesh_Search] And
D3.[Datapoint] <=
C3.[Distribution_Mesh_Search] And
A3.[Maximum_Regularised_Datapoint] = -1)

Group By A3.[Dataset], A3.[Datapoint]

Union All

Select --Coalesce non-exploding/non-imploding
gradient datapoints.

        A4.[Dataset] As [Dataset],

        A4.[Datapoint] As [Datapoint],
```

B4.[Distribution_Mesh_Search] As [Spot_Confidence]

From @Limit_Normalised_Projection_Datapoint_Regulariser A4

Inner Join @Projection_Spot_Confidence_Percentage B4

On (B4.[Dataset] = A4.[Dataset] And B4.[Datapoint] = A4.[Datapoint] And A4.[Datapoint] = A4.[Minimum_Regularised_Datapoint] And A4.[Datapoint] = A4.[Middle_Regularised_Datapoint] And A4.[Datapoint] = A4.[Maximum_Regularised_Datapoint])

--This table variable transforms the regularised probability datapoints into confidence percentages.

--It implements a model phase transition capability which enables a gradual switch between the polynomial probability gradient and the ternary probability step models.

--It achieves this by comparing the size of each parameter density depression, with the @Exploding_Probability_Gradient_Dataset_Range_Limit_Percentage global variable, in order to rectify every exploding probability curve gradients.

Declare @Model_Phase_Transitioned_Projection_Spot_ Confidence_Percentage_Limit_Normalised_Fina l Table ([Dataset] Nvarchar(250), [Datapoint] Float, [Spot_Confidence] Float)

Insert Into @Model_Phase_Transitioned_Projection_Spot_ Confidence_Percentage_Limit_Normalised_Fina l ([Dataset], [Datapoint], [Spot_Confidence])

Select

[Dataset] As [Dataset],

[Datapoint] As [Datapoint],

(Case When [Spot_Confidence] > 100 Then 100 Else (Case When [Spot_Confidence] < 0 Then 0 Else [Spot_Confidence] End) End) As [Spot_Confidence]

From @Model_Phase_Transitioned_Projection_Spot_ Confidence_Percentage_Intermediate

```
Declare
@Model_Phase_Transitioned_Projection_Sprea
d_Confidence_Percentage Table ([Dataset]
Nvarchar(250), [Datapoint] Float,
[Spread_Confidence] Float)

Insert Into
@Model_Phase_Transitioned_Projection_Sprea
d_Confidence_Percentage ([Dataset],
[Datapoint], [Spread_Confidence])

Select

        [Dataset] As [Dataset],

        [Datapoint] As [Datapoint],

        (100 - [Spot_Confidence]) As
[Spread_Confidence]

From
@Model_Phase_Transitioned_Projection_Spot_
Confidence_Percentage_Limit_Normalised_Fina
l

--Some scientists would refer to spread
confidence as 'Energy/Entropy Level' instead.
```

--The following codeblocks load the distribution
mesh search table variable into various

matrices, which correspond to the Michaelian similarity transformation

Declare
@Michaelian_Similarity_Matrix_Cross_Join
Table ([X_Dataset] Nvarchar(250), [Y_Dataset]
Nvarchar(250), [X_Distribution_Mesh_Search]
Float, [Y_Distribution_Mesh_Search] Float)

Insert Into
@Michaelian_Similarity_Matrix_Cross_Join
([X_Dataset], [Y_Dataset],
[X_Distribution_Mesh_Search],
[Y_Distribution_Mesh_Search])

Select

      A.[Dataset] As [X_Dataset],

      B.[Dataset] As [Y_Dataset],

      A.[Spot_Confidence] As
[X_Distribution_Mesh_Search],

      B.[Spot_Confidence] As
[Y_Distribution_Mesh_Search]

From
@Model_Phase_Transitioned_Projection_Spot_
Confidence_Percentage_Limit_Normalised_Fina
l A

```
Inner Join
@Model_Phase_Transitioned_Projection_Spot_
Confidence_Percentage_Limit_Normalised_Fina
l B

        On (B.[Datapoint] = A.[Datapoint])



Declare
@Michaelian_Pair_Dataset_Similarity_Matrix
Table ([X_Dataset] Nvarchar(250), [Y_Dataset]
Nvarchar(250),
[Michaelian_X_Dataset_Similarity] Float)

Insert Into
@Michaelian_Pair_Dataset_Similarity_Matrix
([X_Dataset], [Y_Dataset],
[Michaelian_X_Dataset_Similarity])

Select

        [X_Dataset],

        [Y_Dataset],

        Avg((Case When [X_Dataset] =
[Y_Dataset] Then Null Else ((Case When
[X_Distribution_Mesh_Search] = 0 Then (Case
When [Y_Distribution_Mesh_Search] = 0 Then 1
Else (Case When [X_Distribution_Mesh_Search]
= [Y_Distribution_Mesh_Search] Then 1 Else
(Case When [X_Distribution_Mesh_Search] >
```

[Y_Distribution_Mesh_Search] Then
(([X_Distribution_Mesh_Search] -
[Y_Distribution_Mesh_Search]) /
[X_Distribution_Mesh_Search]) Else
(([X_Distribution_Mesh_Search] -
[Y_Distribution_Mesh_Search]) /
[Y_Distribution_Mesh_Search]) End) End) End)
Else (Case When [X_Distribution_Mesh_Search]
= [Y_Distribution_Mesh_Search] Then 1 Else
(Case When [X_Distribution_Mesh_Search] >
[Y_Distribution_Mesh_Search] Then
(([X_Distribution_Mesh_Search] -
[Y_Distribution_Mesh_Search]) /
[X_Distribution_Mesh_Search]) Else
(([X_Distribution_Mesh_Search] -
[Y_Distribution_Mesh_Search]) /
[Y_Distribution_Mesh_Search]) End) End) End)
* 100) End)) As
[Michaelian_X_Dataset_Similarity]

From
@Michaelian_Similarity_Matrix_Cross_Join

Group By [X_Dataset], [Y_Dataset]

--Any two identical deepsets should be 100%
similar, and any two swapped deepsets (i.e. the
x-axis dataset swapped for the y-axis dataset)
should be inverse.

```
Declare
@Michaelian_Total_Dataset_Similarity_Matrix
Table ([Dataset] Nvarchar(250),
[Michaelian_Total_Dataset_Similarity] Float)

Insert Into
@Michaelian_Total_Dataset_Similarity_Matrix
([Dataset],
[Michaelian_Total_Dataset_Similarity])

Select

        [X_Dataset] As [Dataset],

        Avg(Sqrt(Power([Michaelian_X_Dataset
_Similarity], 2))) As
[Michaelian_Total_Dataset_Similarity]

From
@Michaelian_Pair_Dataset_Similarity_Matrix

Where [Michaelian_X_Dataset_Similarity] Is Not
Null

Group By [X_Dataset]

--Beware that this metric should always be
positive, because there is no pairwise
comparison anymore, but rather multi-
comparison.
```

```
Declare
@Michaelian_Overall_Analysis_Similarity_Matri
x Table ([Analysis] Nvarchar(Max),
[Michaelian_Overall_Analysis_Similarity] Float)

Insert Into
@Michaelian_Overall_Analysis_Similarity_Matri
x ([Analysis],
[Michaelian_Overall_Analysis_Similarity])

Select

        @Analysis_Label As [Analysis],

        Avg([Michaelian_Total_Dataset_Similari
ty]) As [Michaelian_Overall_Analysis_Similarity]

From
@Michaelian_Total_Dataset_Similarity_Matrix




--LOAD STAGE PART TWO:

Select (@Analysis_Label + ':Load Stage Part Two
Started At Around:' + Cast(GetDate() As
Nvarchar(Max))) As [Execution_Progress]
```

--The following codeblock returns all remaining useful data of interest from this algorithm

```sql
--Already loaded --->>> Select * From
@Deepset_Statistical_Significance_Sigma_Band
s Order By [Dataset] Asc,
[Post_Sampling_Sigma_Band] Asc

Select * From @Deepsets Order By
[Deepset_Partition] Asc, [Dataset] Asc

Select * From @Fully_Normalised_Deepsets
Order By [Dataset] Asc,
[Fully_Normalised_Parameter] Asc

Select * From
@Model_Phase_Transitioned_Projection_Spot_
Confidence_Percentage_Limit_Normalised_Fina
l Order By [Dataset] Asc, [Datapoint] Asc

Select * From
@Model_Phase_Transitioned_Projection_Sprea
d_Confidence_Percentage Order By [Dataset]
Asc, [Datapoint] Asc

Select * From
@Michaelian_Pair_Dataset_Similarity_Matrix
Order By [X_Dataset] Asc, [Y_Dataset] Asc
```

```
Select * From
@Michaelian_Total_Dataset_Similarity_Matrix
Order By [Dataset] Asc
```

```
Select * From
@Michaelian_Overall_Analysis_Similarity_Matri
x
```

```
--Finished Progress Report
```

```
Select ('Query Finished At Around:' +
Cast(GetDate() As Nvarchar(Max))) As
[Execution_Progress]
```

```
Select 'If this analysis has taken too much time
to execute with regards to your needs, please
consider increasing the assigned value of the
global variable called
@Projection_Granularity_Global_Variable_Perc
entage, which can be found near the start of
the source code for this query.'
```

```
Select 'ALL GLORY TO GOD!'
```

Example Michaelian Distribution
Probability Curve

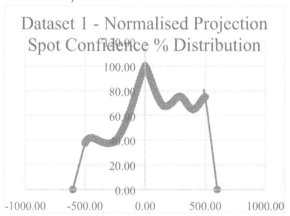

Dataset 1 - Normalised Projection
Spot Confidence % Distribution

My Dream For Probability Theory

I like to dream of a future for humanity, where governmental, corporate, academic, and charitable boardrooms, advisory sessions, team meetings, plans, and reports, no longer suffer from the curse of misunderstandings, bogus reputations, disagreements, or delays. This probability theory of mine, should provide all humanity with a universal, un-biased, understandable, benchmark by which to eradicate these previously mentioned scourges of decision-making, and usher in a new era, of full data literacy and capability. In this case, the intended usage of the two metrics of probability is as follows:

Step 1 – Baselining

You or your responsible subordinate first generates a forecast of a basic mean average datapoint, and then assigns it a confidence value.

Step 2 – Causal Modelling

Causal modelling aims to generate an event aggregating time-series prediction of highly deterministic future states. Managers will need to include event-triggered asset price movements which have start and end dates, each event having/not having leading/trailing profiles, each of which having its own half-life parameter. These profiles should include blunt, straight, concave, convex, and s-curve. Multi-layered if/then/else logic may also be useful. Equations and outputs, from a spreadsheet analysis, should be entered into the causal model simulator. Please see an example below.

The example causal model event below generates a prediction datapoint which is based on deterministic causal modelling. Prediction datapoints should be tightly controlled by accountable management. They are essentially a form of damage limitation on the one hand, and help to rein in emotional human overconfidence on the other hand. Here we calculate the stadium event bar food and drinks revenue:

a. My stadium has 20 bars, each with 5 bar tenders.

b. The game is split into two halves, with a 30 minute window in the middle, as well as at the beginning and end, where customers tend to buy food and drinks.

c. The game lasts for 1 hour.

d. During play, bar staff utilisation is 10%, and at all other times, utilisation is at 100%.

e. Average order value is £5.

f. Average order time is 2 minutes.

g. Therefore, total bar food and drinks revenue for the event is predicted to be: (((20*5*30*3*1)+(20*5*30*2*0.1))*5)/2 = £24,000.

Every prediction should be given a confidence %.

I actually have an algorithm to completely automate this causal modelling step, but it requires the use of ubiquitous, miniaturised, room-temp, very high Q-bit, stable for at least a few minutes, fully interconnected quantum processors. We'll get there by around 2040 to 2060 I should think... I could implement it in T-SQL, but this would be pointless, as the algorithm would be dog-slow on standard digital hardware. Never know though, may be a summer project in a season not too distant from now!

Step 3 – Scenario Modelling

Before you make the crucial decisions in this step, you first need to make sure that you have a significance value which describes the relationships within your sample data, but also another significance value which describes the relationship between any utilised models of prediction (causals). The first metric, **data significance**, measures **data risk** arising from the spread of data in your forecasting mean average model. The second metric, **model significance**, measures **model risk** arising from the spread of limits generated from the various forecasting and/or causal models you are utilising. To compare data significance and model significance you will have to perform a dataset cross-normalisation, as previously outlined.

You then look into your heart, and draw on gut instinct, to assign some value or multiple values in-between the forecast mean average, and the prediction limits (from causal modelling). These are your projection scenarios. These projections should be augmented by a number of other modelling techniques such as a more complex reinforcement learning derived average datapoint (in which case you will need to run at least 50 to 100 simultaneous models in order to ensure significance is fully 'explored'), a PESTELMEMS analysis, using transformer-based machine learning search engine ranking algorithms, in order to boil the internet down into essential pertinent information. Alongside this, deep perception neural networks applied to data feeds from satellites and terrestrial IOT sensors should be included at this stage, in order to monitor and alert to essential changes in the actual physical real-world configuration, which could boost your analysis. A confidence value should 'probably' be calculated for each scenario under consideration. This will help you make better projections.

Instead of step 3, adjacent above, if you like, you can simply set scenario percentiles in between the forecast average datapoint and the predicted datapoint. To calculate the projection scenario datapoint for a specific percentile e.g. +/- 90%, spread normalised confidence % needs to be proved through the use of a parallel mesh search transformation. Essentially you split the dataset range into chunks, each with a sensitivity threshold e.g. 1% (for lean sensitivity), which dictates its size (in this case 1% of the dataset range, for a sensitivity of 1%). Then, for each sub-range chunk, you calculate spread normalised confidence % (percentile), by taking the mean average spread normalised confidence % for the upper and lower bound of that sub-range chunk... Spread normalised confidence % can be calculated by the following equation: (100 minus normalised spot confidence %) for a given datapoint. Then you will be able to return all sub-ranges where the associated percentile meets the criteria for the projection scenario percentile targets, with the proviso that the percentile value within the chunk range is either exactly correct, or if not, then no more than slightly above or below the actual desired projection scenario percentile datapoint, the sensitivity being 1% (or otherwise).

These projection scenario datapoints are your scientifically, artistically, and theologically optimal projections for the future state of your organisation, team, or individual's real-world configuration. You can then describe the probability of a scenario as having a significance of X% i.e. the risk measure, and a confidence of Y% i.e. the reward measure.

Step 4 – Alpha State Reward and Beta State Punishment Learning

If you are less technically minded, focus on the spot confidence metric, as this is the most important. It basically gives a minimum percentage probability for the projected scenarios' datapoints. An adjustable band of +/-1% or similar should be assigned in order to recognise near-hits where you have experienced 'roughly' expected returns/utility (the most probable possible future state).

Alpha and beta are determined by the desired polarity of the metric being projected. If the projection is a positive metric i.e. you want a higher value, then alpha will be above the projected datapoint and beta will be below the projected datapoint. If the projection is a negative metric i.e. you want a lower value, then instead, alpha will be below the projected datapoint and beta will be above the projected datapoint.

Improbable future beta state i.e. marginal returns/utility (a less probable possible future state) occurs when the projected datapoint turns out to be too optimistic, and so we have underperformed. Beta is calculated as a spread confidence %: i.e. (100 minus normalised confidence %) when projection datapoint is below the forecast average, and a spot confidence: i.e. normalised confidence % when the projection datapoint is above the forecast average.

Least probable future alpha state i.e. super returns/utility (the least probable possible future state) occurs when the projected datapoint turns out to be too pessimistic, and so we have overperformed. Alpha is calculated as a spread confidence %: i.e. (100 minus normalised confidence %) when projection datapoint is below the forecast average, and a spot confidence: i.e. normalised confidence % when the projection datapoint is above the forecast average.

Spread Confidence is the reverse simple integral of the normal distribution curve i.e. the depth (from the maximum 100% confidence limit) of the scenario projection datapoint confidence % 'limit'. On the other hand, **Spot Confidence** is the simple integral of the normal distribution curve i.e. the height (from the minimum 0% confidence limit) of the scenario projection datapoint confidence % 'limit'. Finally, **Distribution Confidence** (used for option prioritisation, which is mentioned later in this book) is the total integral of the normal distribution curve i.e. the sum of all unique dataset sample parameter confidence % heights.

Nota Bene: In order to help you understand the concepts and workings of alpha and beta performance possibly more easily, please see the grid below. The reason why the operators below both contain the equal to clause, is because, if you have a confidence of 100%, then there is no distribution or probability. Rather, either you have one sample, or all your samples are the same. Conversely, a confidence of 0% is reserved for projections outside of the sample dataset range. As a result, the forecast average must be shared by both halves of the distribution curve.

Item	Scenario State 1 - Alpha	Scenario State 2 - Alpha	Scenario State 3 - Beta	Scenario State 4 - Beta
Desired Polarity Of the Projection	Positive	Positive	Negative	Negative
Projection Position	Projection Datapoint > Forecast Average	Projection Datapoint <= Forecast Average	Projection Datapoint > Forecast Average	Projection Datapoint <= Forecast Average
Probability Type	Spot	Spread	Spot	Spread
Equation	(Confidence Percentage)	100 - Confidence Percentage	(Confidence Percentage)	100 - Confidence Percentage
Visualisation	Alpha	Alpha	Beta	Beta
	Projection	Average	Projection	Average
	Average	Projection	Average	Projection
	Beta	Beta	Alpha	Alpha

If you haven't already realised, the concepts of alpha and beta are the core embodiment of **Reward and Punishment Learning**. I would suggest that it is probably within your best interests to maximise alpha returns/utility, and minimise beta returns/utility. Expected returns/utility is acceptable I would suppose. The actual machine learning technique entails storing all variables, i.e. global and local, whenever an alpha state or beta state is encountered, as a reminder to the artificial intelligence system that whenever it next experiences the exact same values +/- an adjustable 1% or similar threshold for most of the saved global and local variables e.g. > 80% of them, it should repeat the same decision it made last time when it entered into an alpha state, and avoid the same decision it made last time when it entered into a beta state. I would suggest that you include different time horizons for the assessment or labelling of alpha states and beta states. This would be wise practice, because we know that some decisions/actions don't have their full effect until a long chain of causal events unfolds afterwards. Also, you may in some circumstances experience additional system effectiveness, if you make use of reward and punishment recall retention periods.

*Nota Bene: Be aware that in some special cases, you may encounter what I call an **Envelope Metric**. This is when the metric doesn't have a polarity per-se, but instead is ideally maintained within an 'envelope' i.e. kept within a certain narrow upper and lower limit range of values. I will let you work out how to deal with this type of metric, when it comes to reward and punishment learning, on your own, but essentially, alpha is towards the mean average, and beta is towards either limit, after projecting your scenario.*

Step 5 – Longer Term Scenario Projections

Longer distance (in time usually) projection scenarios can be made by changing the time granularity of sample parameter values e.g. by either recording at a larger granularity of say a month rather than a day, or by simply aggregating more granular data such as days up into synthesised month samples. These longer-term projection scenarios can then be combined with the shorter term projection scenarios in order to generate what I call a fan diagram, or alternatively an error bar plot.

Step 6 – Due Diligence

Where there is a conflict of interest, you can make sure there are no moral abuses going on in critical domain applications, by forcing people to automatically assume the mean average between predicted datapoint and forecast average datapoint, when building their scenario projections. Alternatively, set an organisation-wide or team-wide benchmark upon which to skew the 'trust' between the current forecasting and predicting capabilities within your organisation and/or team. If the accountable management is historically more capable and knowledgeable than the responsible subordinates, then you probably want to choose a benchmark of **greater than** mean average between the predicted datapoint and forecast average datapoint, when the projection scenario datapoint is **above** the forecast average mean; and a benchmark of **less than** mean average between the predicted datapoint and forecast average datapoint, when the projection scenario datapoint is **below** the forecast average mean. On the other hand, if the responsible subordinates are historically more capable and knowledgeable than the accountable management, then you probably want to choose a benchmark of **less than** mean average between the predicted datapoint and forecast average datapoint, when the projection scenario datapoint is **above** the forecast average mean; and a benchmark of **greater than** mean average between the predicted datapoint and forecast average datapoint, when the projection scenario datapoint is **below** the forecast average mean. Otherwise, if there is a capability and knowledge balance or 'harmony' between the two parties, a benchmark somewhere around the mean average would be appropriate, between predicted datapoint and forecast average datapoint.

Decision Making Using Volatility and the Obsidian Metric

This is described in detail in my blog book entitled "...Out Of the Void: Musings On Financial Engineering, Financial Markets, Meta-Economics, and More". Essentially you want to build an Obsidian rank distribution from the probability metrics, in order to prioritise options for decisions, as well as subsequent actioning using decision science in conjunction with prioritisation integrals.

www.ingramcontent.com/pod-product-compliance
Lightning Source LLC
LaVergne TN
LVHW041213050326
832903LV00021B/595